Children and Discipline
A Teacher's Guide

John Wilson and Barbara Cowell

CASSELL

Cassell Educational Limited
Villiers House
41/47 Strand
London WC2N 5JE

First published 1990

British Library Cataloguing in Publication Data
Wilson, John, *1928–*
    Children and discipline.
    1. Children. Behaviour modifications: Manuals, for
    parents
    I. Title   II. Cowell, Barbara   III. Series
    649.64

    ISBN 0-304-32282-2
    ISBN 0-304-32266-0 pbk

Typeset by Colset Private Limited, Singapore
Printed and bound in Great Britain by
Biddles Ltd, Guildford and King's Lynn

Contents

General Editor's Foreword to the Series

The books in this series were written in response to the conviction that all those who are concerned with education should have a deep interest in the nature of children's learning. Teaching and policy decisions ultimately depend on an understanding of individual personalities accumulated through experience, observation and research. Too often in recent years, decisions on the management of education have had little to do with the realities of children's lives, and too often the interest shown in the performance of teachers, or in the content of the curriculum, has not been balanced by an interest in how children respond to either. The books in this series are based on the conviction that children are not fundamentally different from adults, and that we understand ourselves better by our insight into the nature of children.

The books are designed to appeal to *all* those who are interested in education and take it as axiomatic that anyone concerned with human nature, culture or the future of civilization is interested in education; in the individual process of learning, as well as what can be done to help it. While each book draws on recent findings in research, and is aware of the latest developments in policy, each is written in a style that is clear, readable and free from the jargon that has undermined much scholarly writing, especially in such a relatively new field of study.

Although the audience to be addressed includes all those concerned with education, the most important section of the audience is made up of professional teachers, the teachers who continue to learn and grow and who need both support and stimulation. Teachers are very busy people, whose energies are taken up in coping with difficult circumstances. They deserve material that is stimulating, useful and free of jargon and that is in tune with the practical realities of classrooms.

Each book is based on the principle that the study of education is a discipline in its own right. There was a time when the study of the principles of learning and the individual's response to his or her environment was a collection of parts of other disciplines – history, philosophy, linguistics, sociology and psychology. That time is assumed to be over and the books address those who are interested in the study of children and how they respond to their environment. Each book is written both to enlighten the reader and to offer practical help to develop understanding. They therefore not only contain accounts of what we understand about children, but also illuminate these accounts by a series of examples, based on observation of practice. These examples are designed not as a series of rigid steps to be followed, but to show the realities on which the insights are based.

Most people, even educational researchers, agree that research on children's learning has been most disappointing, even when it has not been completely missing. Apart from the general lack of a 'scholarly' educational tradition, the inadequacies of such study come about because of the fear of approaching such a complex area as children's inner lives. Instead of answering curiosity with observation, much educational research has attempted to reduce the problem to simplistic solutions, by isolating a particular hypothesis and trying to improve it, or by trying to focus on what is easy and 'empirical'. These books try to clarify the real complexities of the problem, and are willing to be speculative. The real disappointment with educational research, however, is that it is very rarely read or used. The people most at home with children are often unaware that helpful insights can be offered to them. The study of children and the understanding that comes from self-knowledge are too important to be left to obscurity. In the broad sense real 'research' is carried out by all those engaged in the task of teaching or bringing up children.

All the books share a conviction that the inner worlds of children repay close attention, and that much subsequent behaviour and attitudes depend upon the early years. The books also share the conviction that children's natures are not markedly different from those of adults, even if they are more honest about themselves. The process of learning is reviewed as the individual's close and idiosyncratic involvement in events, rather than the passive reception of, and processing of, information.

General Editor's Preface

There is always a tension between teaching and learning, a tension most acutely seen in the everyday circumstances of school classrooms. It is acknowledged that the dissemination of the National Curriculum, however carefully it is detailed, depends on the way that teachers interact with pupils. In few places are the relationships between human beings more significant and sometimes more intense than in the classroom. 'Discipline' is not just an extra dimension to the practices of schools, and the control of large numbers of people by a few. It is at the heart of all professional relationships, a matter of interest to all engaged in teaching and learning.

'Discipline' is a word associated closely with difficulties. It is the traumas that some teachers undergo, and the threats that they face, that make the concept of discipline of interest to the government and to the press. Such concern with an extreme example of one of the peculiarities of the classroom is shown in the Elton Report.[1] This report, typically, reacts to the problems of discipline and highlights them. Within its recommendations for improved classroom management it does not seriously question *why* teachers should be faced by such extreme circumstances, by such threats and by a need to steel themselves as if for battle.

The Elton Report highlights a particular problem that all teachers need to know how to deal with. But discipline is a highly complex issue. At one level it is manifested in classroom management, in personality, expectations and rules. It also depends, as this book shows, on the nature of authority, and authority manifested not only in school but in society as a whole.

The Elton Report does reveal the importance of the concept of the 'ethos' of the school. 'It is also important to find ways of creating an atmosphere in school in which pupils do not even think of being aggressive towards teachers' (p. 11). The report talks about the importance of personal and social education and pays attention to the appearance of schools. Thereby it acknowledges, even in extreme cases, the more general problem of social and personal authority. Recent research reports make it clear how important the differences between different schools are, in terms of their ethos and their results.[2] The concepts of discipline and authority are at the root of the ways in which different schools manifest how they work.

The importance of institutional ethos lies in it being a positive, not a negative, factor. We might associate discipline with repression; we tend to think of ethos in terms of enlightenment and communication. Ethos is there to encourage the best rather than suppress the worst, to explain the need for order rather than blindly to impose it. This gives pupils a real sense of what they are trying to achieve as individuals, within society. Pupils, after all, wish to have clear rules that deal with everyone fairly.[3]

This book has three major themes that are of practical consequence to teachers in any sphere. It draws attention to the close relationship between authority and discipline. It shows that the really large question depends on the nature of the imposition of and obedience to authority and why this should come about. The second major theme of the book is a celebration of the significance of pupils as thinking people. It acknowledges the importance of the purpose of schools, a purpose in which pupils clearly share. The book also celebrates the teacher who is thinking about what he or she is doing. The book draws attention to the need for teachers to be able to stand back and reflect on their own practices. Both pupils and teachers, therefore, need some sense of self-awareness to question and understand the nature of authority.

Discipline and authority are social matters. They are attempts to bring order to the chaos of complex relationships. To this extent the school is a microcosm of society. Every individual in a school can face traumas as a result of unfairness. Many teachers undergo very difficult personal circumstances in trying to acknowledge, and come to terms with, the needs of all the individuals that face them.[4] It is amazing what we expect teachers to do, in their response to so many different needs often badly expressed but all demanding attention. Understanding the nature of discipline and authority helps to understand how these individual needs can be dealt with.

All teachers, therefore, need to understand the context of the school in its society. They need to understand why rules come about and how a sense of purpose can be engendered. Teachers also need practical support. This book, by reflecting on this fundamental question, gives teachers an important aid to their practice. Nothing is more practical than thinking around a problem we all face. Looking at the question of authority shows that the solution to the real problems is not to be found in more will-power but in a whole school policy that is based on greater understanding.

REFERENCES

1 Department of Education and Science. *Discipline in Schools*. Report of the Committee of Enquiry chaired by Lord Elton. (HMSO, London, 1989).
2 See, for example, P. Mortimore *et al. School Matters: The Junior Years*. (Open Books, Wells, 1988).
3 C. Cullingford. 'School rules and children's attitudes to discipline.' *Educational Research*, **30**, no. 1, 1988, pp. 3-8.
4 K.A. Cronk. *Teacher–Pupil Conflict in Secondary Schools*. (Falmer Press, Lewes, 1987).

Authors' Preface

It hardly needs saying that problems about children and discipline are not only of perennial importance and faced by all educators and societies in the world, but also particularly noticeable in societies that, like our own, are deeply uncertain about how those problems ought to be solved. In the daily life and experience of all teachers and parents, practical and painful difficulties arise all the time: how to maintain discipline without unnecessary harshness, how to encourage reasonable moral thought and behaviour without indoctrination, how to keep order and control in the family or the classroom without adopting a pose of infallibility or omnipotence. Few of us need to be reminded of the importance of the topic.

Less obvious, however, and directly relevant to the structure of this book, is a crucial point that we are apt to shy away from. In the hurly-burly of the classroom or the family - let alone the football stadium or the vandalized housing estate - we long for some quick answer, some immediate cure or recipe. We have to face the fact that there is no such thing. (If there were, there would be little point in writing books about it.) Our difficulties, and the difficulties of our children and young people, stem from very basic causes; we have to understand these fully if we are to have any chance of success. We have, therefore, to apply not just our determination, or our kindness, or our willingness to act. We have to deploy our intelligence in order to understand.

It is a central part of the thesis of this book that such understanding is *not* a matter for psychological or sociological or any other kind of academic experts. It is a matter of our gaining a proper grasp of: (a) the *concepts* that we ought to have under such titles as 'authority', 'discipline', 'rules', 'morality' and so forth; and (b) the *hang-ups* that we ourselves have about these things - the prejudices, fantasies, unseen emotions and other forces that too often control our behaviour and our thinking. Briefly, what we require is neither a vast quantity of scholarly research that will eventually 'tell us the answer', for the 'answer' must come from our own minds and hearts; nor an enhancement of our own efforts of will-power and conscientiousness, for any such efforts must be properly guided by understanding. Rather, we need a kind of sophisticated common sense, an awareness of our own thinking and feeling.

Consequently we have not, in this book, made constant reference to what goes on in schools, families and other contexts in which the notion of authority and discipline come into question. The reader (whether or not a practising teacher or a parent) will have plenty of experience of his or her own on which to draw; and though both the authors are themselves practising teachers and parents, it would be presumptuous of us to suggest that the reader lacks such experience. What we do suggest, however, is that (perhaps just for lack of time) the reader may not have thought thoroughly enough about the concepts. So we aim here to help the reader *stand back* - sometimes quite far back - from his or her daily experience, and think more deeply about the concepts and feelings that generate the experience. Only such thought will ultimately improve the practical situation.

'Philosophy' and 'psychology' are grand names for the disciplines that can help us here, and in practising them we are up against certain enemies that attack all of us. Once more, these enemies are not lack of will-power or lack of intellectual talent. They are, rather, such things as fantasy, prejudices, predetermined attitudes to which we cling in order to feel safe, and a whole set of unconscious emotions that distract us from reason. The relevant virtues here are patience, seriousness, carefulness, the ability to tolerate doubt, the desire to follow arguments carefully and a kind of self-awareness. The authors cannot pose as 'experts' in all this: the best we can hope for is that we can, together with the reader, try to make a bit more sense of the whole area.

In Part A we shall look directly and in a down-to-earth way at the concepts of authority, discipline and other connected ideas, so that we can at least start by getting a clear understanding of these. Then in Part B we shall try to say something helpful about how, in point of fact, we *feel* about them: what attitudes we and other people have in this area, and how they can be changed in the direction of reason. We believe this to be more than half the battle, and when either of us – as very often happens! – fails at home or at school in this area, we can nearly always trace it to some failing of understanding or feeling *within ourselves*. So what may seem 'abstract' or 'academic' in our discussion is, in fact, the most 'practical' way forward: the faults are within us (not just in 'society', or due to original sin, or the government, or 'the modern world', or 'the system'), and can only be cured by looking within. In Part C we describe one or two practical methods that seem directly relevant to the area, in the hope that teachers and others will find them useful; but here in particular we would stress the point that teachers and parents are – once their understanding and feeling are sound – the best 'experts', and no doubt other practical methods will occur to them which are just as important as those we suggest in this book.

Problems about authority and discipline are, as we said at the beginning, a running sore in all societies. The sore can be healed, but only by prolonged and careful thought. We hope that what follows will help others in the same predicament as ourselves to think more clearly.

J.B.W. and B.C.
Oxford, 1990

Acknowledgements

We should like to acknowledge the fact that we have drawn on material published elsewhere, particularly in *Philosophy and Practical Education* (Routledge, London, 1977), *Discipline and Moral Education* (NFER, Windsor, 1981), *Practical Methods of Moral Education* (Heinemann, London, 1972) and *Lord of the Flies* by William Golding (Faber and Faber Ltd, London). We also express thanks to numerous critics, in particular to Cedric Cullingford and Nancy Swift.

Introductory Dialogue

This is a word-for-word transcript of a talk between one of the authors and one of his pupils, back in 1960, when the author was in charge of a boarding house at a school in Canterbury, with 80 pupils to look after of ages from 13 to 18. The boy, Peter, was 14 years old, of about average academic ability. He had got into various kinds of trouble over the previous few months, sometimes bullying pupils smaller than he was, being late for class and rude to some of the staff, not putting his clothes away, and so on. Like quite a few pupils sometimes labelled as 'troublemakers' or 'against authority', he was quick and articulate beyond his years, very well able to put up a defence of his behaviour and to argue his own case (something most of us are quick to do). Quite a lot of the central issues about authority emerged in the talk.

J.B.W.: Now look here Peter, I really must talk to you seriously about your behaviour. I mean, it really won't do, being rude to Mr X and Miss Y, you know perfectly well that –

Peter: I don't know perfectly well, Mr X really asked for it, he told me to turn up at 10 o'clock and there was no good reason why I should – after all –

J.B.W.: Hang on, I don't want to discuss what Mr X tells you to do, the point is that he's a teacher here and in authority, so you've got to do what he tells you whether you like it or not.

P.: What, even if he tells me to jump in the lake?

J.B.W.: Well, he wouldn't do anything as silly as that, he's –

P.: So you're saying I haven't got to do as he says when it's silly?

J.B.W.: It's not your business to decide when it's silly.

P.: I shan't obey just because he has power over me. Anyway, he doesn't have much. I didn't want to come to this school and he can't make me do things. Neither can you. I'll just walk out if I have to.

J.B.W.: Well, you can't quite do that at your age. Where would you go? You have to stay at school till you're 16 anyway. Won't you trust us to do our best for you till then? We don't want to squash you, just to educate you till you're grown up and can do as you like.

P.: Who gave you that power? Not me. I don't see why I should obey people just because they're bigger and older.

J.B.W.: What about your father?

P.: Not even him, I didn't ask to be born or live in his house, it's not fair.

J.B.W.: OK, but you *are* living in his house, and you're in this school, so shouldn't you keep the rules? After all they're fairly sensible. You've been bullying Smith and Jones – how would you like it if you were bullied? My job is to stop that sort of thing.

P.: Well, OK, I might agree to that. But you've never asked me, just given me orders.

J.B.W.: Haven't I tried to help you here?

P.: H'm, well, yes, you did lend me some money and got me out of trouble with Mr Z. I'm not against you, really, but I still don't see why I have to fit into the system.

J.B.W.: But wherever you were you'd have to fit into *some* system. Even if you ran away to sea – captains of ships exercise a lot of power over the sailors.

P.: But I want to choose what system.

J.B.W.: But you can't have exactly what system you like; it's like when you play cricket, you can't be batting all the time, sometimes you have to take your turn fielding – there are other people besides yourself, you know.

P.: OK, I see that. But somehow I feel – you wouldn't understand – I expect your father was nice to you, mine just shouts at me and doesn't explain things.

J.B.W.: Yes, but even when they're explained people still want to disobey. I mean you know quite well it's a damned nuisance if you leave your clothes lying around, someone else has to pick them up. And you try being a teacher with the pupils coming in late all the time! Think about it.

P.: You say 'think about it', but how can I when nobody ever explains it and talks about it? This school ought to educate us properly about all this. All the teachers do is just exercise power – when they can.

That last remark deserves repetition: 'This school ought to educate us properly about all this. All the teachers do is just exercise power – when they can'.

As far as that school was concerned, Peter's remark was fair enough; and it may apply to other schools. We are not saying that this is the teachers' fault. Teachers (as we see it, anyway) are an oppressed class: they have to work very hard for not much money, and they are constantly under pressure not only from pupils and 'society' (the teenage or 'pop' culture), but also from parents, local and central authorities, advisers, inspectors, the demands of examination systems and educational theorists, all telling them – kindly or unkindly – what they ought to do. They do not always have enough power or scope to do the job, and are often not supported by the pupils' homes as much as they should be. Nevertheless, Peter has a point.

The point is this. In the past, we have (by and large) simply *assumed* that the teacher (backed by the home and by society) should enjoy a certain authority, and that everyone – including the pupils – agreed to this. The authority may have been based on some sort of consensus about morality, good behaviour, middle-class values or a Christian way of life, or whatever, but it was largely taken for granted. Nowadays, in many parts of the world (and increasingly all over the world), that is no longer true. The whole business of authority is now controversial, unclear and troublesome. Pupils behave very badly sometimes (perhaps often), and make the teacher's life hell. Discipline is not always what it should be, despite the teacher's best efforts. Pupils come from different cultures, races, creeds and sets of values – there is not now the general consensus that there was. Not only pupils but teachers and people in society generally are, understandably, very worried about this, and teachers are in the front line, bearing most of the brunt. Teachers try to 'exercise power – when they can', as Peter says, but often they cannot.

Something important follows from this, which we want to deal

3

with in this book. It is obvious enough that, simply in order to get any serious educational business done in schools, we shall have to ensure that teachers have enough authority (and power) to run schools properly. But it is also obvious that they will not be able to do this unless there is some *rational agreement* about the nature and scope of that authority. We cannot put the clock back: we have to think and talk to each other and negotiate, and reach a proper *understanding* of what authority is and how it ought to be used in schools. Now once we talk in this way – rather than just saying that teachers must be given more power – it also becomes clear that *the whole business of authority is an essential topic for discussion with pupils and for their education.* In other words, the understanding of notions like authority, power, discipline and so on, their proper use and the kinds of feelings we have about them, are not just things we – the teachers – have to get straight and then simply bring to bear on the pupils. We have (also) to make sure that the pupils *understand them* (not just *suffer* them, as it were). As Peter says, 'this school ought to educate us properly about all this'.

We think this has a claim to be one of the most important, perhaps the most important, aspects or departments of education. The idea is not new. More than 2000 years ago, Plato wrote this (in his *Laws*):

> When we abuse or commend the upbringing of individual people and say that one of us is educated and the other uneducated, we sometimes use this latter term of men who have in fact had a thorough education – one directed towards petty trade or the merchant shipping business or something like that. But I take it that for the purpose of the present discussion we are not going to treat this sort of thing as 'education': what we have in mind is education from childhood in virtue, a training which produces a keen desire to become a perfect citizen *who knows how to rule and be ruled as justice requires.*

This is as true as it ever was. Plato, like ourselves and like Peter, lived at a time when consensus had broken down, so that educators had to go back to square one and work things out from first principles. From first principles: which means, *not* from any partisan ideology of our own. For any such ideology (a point we shall be talking about later on) is bound to be questioned by pupils, and will not simply be swallowed whole.

So in this book we have to go back to the beginning. What *are* authority, discipline, power? What authority *should* teachers have? How do pupils – and adults, come to that – *feel* about authority and power? What emotional battles do we and they fight inside ourselves about it? How far do pupils understand it, or how far can they understand it? How can we become clearer about such notions as rules, contracts, discipline and the whole business of negotiating authority with pupils within a system of compulsory education? We shall take a hard look at these issues in Parts A and B. In Part C we shall consider one or two practical methods that might help to solve some of our problems, and that follow from some of the considerations in the first two parts.

In thinking about such things (as always in thinking about education), we have to do two things. We have to be able to move from (a) the basic principles of reason and understanding which alone can clarify the idea of authority and its proper use, to (b) what actually goes on in pupils' heads, how they think and talk and behave; and then back again to (a), in order to see how the general principles can be used to put pupils' feelings in better shape; and then back again to (b), those feelings themselves, so that we know just what to say to pupils at particular times, how to handle individual cases. We move back and forth, in other words, from 'theory' to 'practice'. Most teachers are very familiar with practice: they meet it every day in overwhelming quantity. So a high percentage of this book involves inviting the reader to take a step from practice to the theory, the basic principles. But at the same time, in order to preserve the link with practice, with how pupils actually think and feel, we shall quote some dialogues and responses from pupils that (we hope) will remind the reader that we are talking about something real, about concepts and feelings that actually dominate the minds of real people, not just about 'abstract philosophy'.

We cannot pretend that getting a proper grasp on these ideas, and then putting them into effective practice, is easy. (If it was, the whole business of politics and personal relationships – not only in schools but in society generally – would be much better done than in fact it is.) But it is possible, provided one has the patience and desire to be clear. As we shall see, becoming clear is not a matter so much of intellectual talent as of psychological maturity. We have to lay aside our particular reactions and emotions – our 'hang-ups' – about authority, and look more closely at the facts, the logical facts about the concepts and ideas, the emotional facts about ourselves and our pupils, and the practical facts about what actually goes on in schools. Desirable change will only come about in this, as in most other vital educational matters, not by some stroke of the administrative pen wielded by central government, but by the inevitably slow process of increased clarity and understanding.

Part A
Discipline, Authority and Connected Ideas

The concept denoted by 'authority' is central to all forms of human life, not only to education, and we need to understand it fully before we can ground our educational and social practice on a firm and permanent basis. There are two important points to be made right at the start.

First, authority is one of a whole set of concepts which interconnect, and we need some understanding of them all. Others include the ideas marked by discipline, punishment, rules and contract. We shall have something to say about all these, and we have divided the text under different headings, but we hope to make the interconnections clear. We are trying to get a grip on the whole business, remembering, as we have already hinted, that this is not just for the benefit of our own thinking, but that it represents a subject matter that we have to explain to our pupils – in just the same way as we have to be clear about the subject matter of mathematics, science, history or anything else if we are to transmit it to our pupils effectively.

Secondly, to get this grip – and we shall have more to say about this point later – it may be helpful to us to recognize, in advance, two basic postures. Most or all of us (having suffered from or benefited from being under authority as children ourselves) have two mixed-up feelings inside us: (a) sometimes we feel *in favour of* authority generally, perhaps identifying with parental or other authorities, frightened of chaos and anarchy, in need of security, 'right answers' and clear rules that are strictly enforced; (b) sometimes we *rebel against* authority, resenting those set in authority over us, and over others. Some of us may be more inclined to feel (a), and others to feel (b); indeed, there are social and political climates that tend towards one or the other direction at various times (we may identify with 'the establishment' or with 'the underdogs').

These feelings stem from the childish parts within our own minds, and we have to learn not to yield too quickly to them. The truth (as we shall try to show) is that authority and its connected concepts are in themselves neither 'good' nor 'bad': they are inevitable in human life if we want to do any kind of business with other people. They have a function that can (if we keep our heads) be purely reasonable or sensible, and once we are clear what the function is, we can calmly and intelligently discuss the sort of authority (rules, discipline, etc.) that fulfils the function we have in mind (in our case, the business of education). As we shall see, the feelings are in children very obvious; but it is equally important to recognize them in ourselves. Such recognition, even if it is only partial, will save us a lot of unnecessary passion and prejudice.

CHAPTER 1
Authority

We are going to start by approaching the notion of authority obliquely, via the notion of punishment. Here the psychological temperature is at its highest (which is why we want to start here). Remembering what we said a little earlier, we shall recognize in ourselves the feeling that people ought to get what they deserve, that crime ought to be punished, that offenders ought not to be allowed to get away with it. This feeling may sometimes be extremely strong and passionate. On the other hand, we may also feel – and perhaps the more tender-minded and 'caring' of us are more likely to feel this – that punishment is something horrible, objectionable, in itself unfair, certainly unpleasant, something at least we ought to get rid of as far as possible. Now consider the following argument.

Anything that could seriously be called a 'society' or 'social group', as against a collection of hermits who happen to be living in the same area, involves some kind of interaction between its members. 'Interaction' here does not mean that they just bump up against each other like physical objects, but that they engage in some rule-following activity – even if, as perhaps in the case of a seminar or a tea-party, the activity consists only or chiefly of linguistic communication. There will therefore be rules or norms that are commonly subscribed to, whether or not they are codified, overtly agreed and stated beforehand, or contracted for.

A breach of these rules must, at least characteristically if not in every case, be taken to entail the enforcement of some disadvantage on the breaker. If this were not so, we should not be able to identify them as rules prohibiting X and enjoining Y, rather than enjoining X and prohibiting Y; or we should not be able to identify them as *rules* at all, as against wishes, pious hopes, generalizations about human behaviour, or descriptions of some other-worldly ideal. A social rule enjoining X exists only if, when people fail to perform X, something that is characteristically a disadvantage is normally enforced on them.

Various words may be in place for the *type* of disadvantage – punishment, penalty, sanctions, etc. – as well as for the *form* of disadvantage – ostracism, imprisonment, exile. Not all these disadvantages will be *painful* (going to prison does not involve pain), but they will all be characteristically 'bad things', or they would not be disadvantages but rewards. Thus loss of liberty is, characteristically, a 'bad thing'; although people may sometimes, even often, find that a situation where they are told what to do is more pleasant than a situation where they can do what they want, they must in general wish to retain the option of liberty as long as they continue to see themselves as human agents. Further, whether or not the group gives some of its members particular authority to interpret and enforce the rules and disadvantages, the disadvantages will in every case occur by reason or in virtue of the rules that constitute and govern that group's interaction. That the group subscribes to these rules, or that the rules are in force, logically entails disadvantages to rule-breakers, whether or not these disadvantages are properly called 'punishments' inflicted by special authorities.

In English we speak of 'punishment' in reference to the common and criminal law, and in reference to some institutions with limited sovereignty (for example, schools). With games, and (perhaps) generally in cases where we wish to avoid the implication of moral blame, we prefer to speak of 'penalties'. Elsewhere we may talk of 'sanctions' or, more vaguely, of 'being made to suffer for' a breach of rules (for example, of social etiquette). Not all languages make these distinctions, which may indeed sometimes seem arbitrary: *poena* in Latin, for instance, covers a wider range than our 'punishment'. The question thus arises of whether we are trying to 'justify punishment' in reference to the particular (and, it may be thought, in some degree arbitrary) range of instances for which we use the word punishment (and not penalty, sanctions, etc.) or whether we are trying to 'justify' some more general concept.

If some more general concept is at stake, it is presumably the concept of being (as we have called it) disadvantaged in virtue of rules governing social interaction. But we have seen that such disadvantaging is logically entailed by the notion of social interaction. What could it mean to 'justify punishment (disadvantaging)'? Perhaps some such question as 'why should we have any form of social interaction and rules at all?' might be coherently raised (although we doubt this), but it would be necessary to raise such a question in order to make any sense of justifying punishment *as a whole*. More probably a person who, in real life, protests against or demands justification for punishment objects to one or other of the *kinds* of punishments, rules, authorities or systems in force; but this is a different story. This person might also be led to raise questions about the whole conceptual apparatus of which punishment is part – the whole 'basis of authority', as it might be called – and *some* of these questions, as we shall see below, are both intelligible and important. But that is also a different story.

If, on the other hand, we are interested solely in the specific concept of punishment as the word is used by English speakers, it will be difficult to know how to proceed. Supposing that we dismantled the legal system of judges, codified laws, specified penalties and so on, then plainly there would still remain most or at least some of the forms of social interaction, with rules and ensuing disadvantages, even if these disadvantages were not formally administered in courts of law. The same criteria as those commonly listed by philosophers for 'punishment' would pertain: disadvantages would still be given by the social group for breaches of the rules. Whether or not we would continue to call these punishments, rather than penalties, sanctions, etc., seems to us an open question, and not a very interesting one. Certainly they might be just as harsh, or perhaps harsher. Laws and school rules may be severe, but the sanctions or penalties imposed by mobs, bullies and even peer groups may well be more so. Arguments for or against the specific form of sanctions that seems to be implied by 'punishment' – perhaps a comparatively high degree of formalization, or codification – would be heavily dependent on empirical facts. Off-hand one might be inclined to suppose that the degree of institutionalization implied would improve clarity at least, and hence (other things being equal) be a more desirable form than the more unpredictable forces of codified law in general. But however that may be, we are now clearly involved in a discussion of the best *kinds* of sanctions or disadvantages, not what is commonly taken as 'the justification of punishment'.

This seems to be more than just a social matter. In so far as we, even alone or on a desert island, seriously propose to ourselves ends or goals and rules for achieving them, to that extent we shall necessarily blame ourselves when we fail through our own fault. We shall feel remorse or regret, guilt or shame – we might even talk, more or less metaphorically, of our 'punishing ourselves'. This goes *together with* enthusiasm for the enterprise, not against it or as an alternative strategy to it. Success and failure, and hence in a broad sense rewards and punishments, cannot be expelled from human life. An individual or society may, of course, change the norms (just as, in the way we saw above, the types of sanctions may be changed), and one way of doing this is to take away their sanctions, which at once removes their status as norms. For instance, if being a nuisance in school or society characteristically results in a person's receiving more attention and care (support from counsellors and welfare services, and so on) rather than some disadvantage, then there is no longer an operative norm or rule – although there may be one on paper – against 'being a nuisance'. The norm has in effect become just a pious hope. This sort of situation does, we think, pertain in many schools today; and perhaps also, to no inconsiderable degree, in society at large. It is as if we are no longer sure of the actions we wish to bring under the whole mechanism of *justice*, and this may have the effect of making us lose our grip on the concept of justice itself and on its attendant concepts, of which punishment is one.

For much the same reason there are two other notions (among many), generally denoted by the terms authority and institution, that cannot be ignored. Any society or interacting group of rational creatures must have a common decision procedure – indeed this can be taken as a defining characteristic of a society. The notion of authority presupposes some sort of normative order. But it is also presupposed by it, and it is not true that we can conceive of a society of highly moral beings living together amicably out of respect for a moral law and for each other as rational beings, without anyone being in authority, and without anyone being thought of as an authority. The reason is not that people are inherently non-angelic or bloody minded, but that in order to *express* their amicable dispositions and have respect for each other such beings would need decision procedures and authorities to operate them. If you change the notion of 'normative order' into actual cases of things that these beings might *do* – play cricket, hold debates, run railways, or whatever – the point becomes clear. Authorities (referees, arbitrators, umpires, etc.) are necessary, not just to punish vice, but also to provide clarity in those rule-governed activities. 'The editor's decision is final' not, or not only, because somebody has to mark down incompetent entries, but because it has to be clear what counts as winning the competition. In the same sort of way (the argument need not be put again) the structural contexts that incorporate and clothe these activities – that is, 'institutions' – are also inevitable.

Certainly such considerations as these call certain beliefs (for example, anarchism) into question. Someone who says that he or she wants no rules and punishments *at all*, or the abolition of ('alienating') institutions *in general*, or the complete removal of *any* kind of authority, may have to think twice. But we cannot stop here. People who are morally concerned about punishments, authorities and so on are concerned about *something*, or rather about many things. For there are all sorts of questions we can still raise. The most useful thing we can do here is to say something about some of the particular questions that are likely to be in the minds of teachers and other educators, in relation to what has been said above.

It may still seem as if the conceptual points we have made convey no more than the bleak message, 'you must obey authority'. And does this not have the very unpleasant implications marked by such phrases as unquestioning obedience, conformism, authoritarian regimes and so on? Does it not lead directly to the horrors sometimes perpetrated by those who, like the Nazis, slavishly and uncritically do what they are told? How can we accept these conceptual points (assuming them to be correct) while at the same time educating our children to think for themselves and question authority? How can it be possible both to obey and to challenge?

It may seem at first sight as if the whole idea of 'questioning authority' is somehow contradictory. If one has authority, the implication is that one is and ought to be, at least characteristically, obeyed *whether or not* one's *particular* commands are thought by the individual to be wise, or pleasant, or on other grounds acceptable. Otherwise there would be no difference between an authority and an adviser. The authority of a ship's captain rests on his being obeyed, at least in regard to the ship's management, irrespective of the views of this or that sailor. There is one sense, therefore, in which 'unquestioning obedience' is required by the very notion of authority, just as such obedience, in certain task-like situations, constitutes part of what it is to be well-disciplined. Certainly if there were too many cases of challenge or disobedience, we should hesitate to say that there was any authority (or any discipline) at all.

This will only seem alarming and difficult if we persist in regarding 'authority' as equivalent to one particular set of power-holders or 'authorities', rather as we might identify 'morality' with the particular *mores* of our own society, or 'religion' with the particular religious beliefs and institutions with which we happen to be familiar. Of course we can question, challenge, disobey or dispense entirely with these particular manifestations. But we cannot hope to do without some manifestation – not, at least, as long as we remain human beings and interact socially with each other. Just as it is a conceptual truth that human beings must accept some authority and obey it if they are to get anything done, so it is also conceptually true that questions will inevitably arise about whether particular authorities are legitimate, whether their scope is properly delimited, whether the form and methods by which they operate are as good as we can make them, and so forth.

This is, or ought to be, entirely familiar ground to us. It is roughly similar to saying that, on the one hand, we must abide by whatever the rules of the game are if we are to play games at all, but that, on the other hand, we need sometimes – perhaps often – to think about what sorts of games to play, what rules it would be best to have, whether to have referees or just books of rules, and all the other matters that we need to get straight. Or it is like saying that, on the one hand, there must be some sort of government (sovereign body, set of decision-makers) if we are to act together as a society at all, but that, on the other hand, we need contexts in which we can keep a watching brief on, and often revise, the form or constitution of the government, the delimitation of its sovereignty, or the particular people we want to have as decision-makers.

It is important to note that, even when we engage in this process of reconsideration and revision, we do not thereby step outside of the notion of authority altogether. Suppose that, while nominally under the authority of occupying Nazis, we decide to form a resistance movement. Then, not only are we proposing to substitute one authority for another (the Free French for the Nazis), rather than to get rid of authority altogether, but also *in the process* of deciding this, of *forming* the movement (with its leaders, rules, discipline and so on), we accept some authority. In such a case the authority might be the commands of a particular person (General de Gaulle), or something rather more vague, such as 'the will of the French people'. Simply because our activity is collective and purposive, because we are doing things together for a common end, we have to accept some decision procedure. Again, if pupils in school decided to rebel against the teachers' authority, some other authority would inevitably arise – not only after the success of the rebellion, but in order to carry the rebellion through. Perhaps the pupils would meet and abide by a democratic vote; perhaps they would accept the lead of the strongest and most vociferous. But they would have to accept something.

Of course sensible societies or social groups make proper arrangements for the business of revision. Instead of allowing a free-for-all in which the strongest or most persuasive party is likely to win power, they institutionalize conflicts of opinion and desire: that is, they provide some sort of mechanism or procedure which their members agree to use – for instance, to vote rather than assassinate, or to advance arguments rather than to throw bombs. Agreement about these ultimate decision procedures is crucial. The alternatives to sincere agreement and negotiation within accepted rules are either mindless conformity or some sort of civil war.

In educating pupils to raise questions and be critical about particular manifestations of authority, the most important thing is to provide proper contexts in which this can be done, or perhaps one should say, to allow and encourage the pupils to create and abide by contexts they themselves opt for – since it is more than half the battle to get them to see that the serious 'questioning of authority' itself involves obedience to rules. The task is to show them, or let them come to grasp, that rules and authority are logically required by human co-operation, and not simply imposed from outside in one particular form by one particular set of people (teachers, parents, society or whoever). Success in this task will almost certainly involve giving pupils a good deal of freedom to gain the experiences necessary to grasp the point – although not letting them go as far as the children in Golding's *Lord of the Flies*. Just talking about it is not enough: serious thinking tends to be promoted by actual responsibility, and by taking the consequences of one's own errors.

Are there not some general principles that should guide us (and our pupils) when we are 'questioning authority' in these contexts? What sorts of reasons could we have for setting up one particular manifestation of authority (together with its attendant rules and sanctions) rather than another? Ought our regimes to be more 'democratic' or 'authoritarian', or to involve more 'participation' or 'pupil power'? As these fashionable terms suggest, there are certainly some general pressures – climates of opinion or feeling, as it were – that affect the running of educational institutions in various ways. Can we say anything sensible about all this?

The first and perhaps most important thing to be said is that any overall or *a priori* preference for a particular style or regime – authoritarian, democratic or whatever – is likely to be doctrinaire. As our examples show, everything depends on *what sort of interaction* we want to take place, on what sort of business we want to conduct, what our particular purposes are. The style or regime suitable for an army or a ship of war will differ from that suitable for running a railway, a factory or a school. Moreover, it is clear that much depends on the people themselves: their age, or maturity, common sense or natural tendencies. Thus it would be ludicrous to attempt a democratic regime for young children in war-time: first, because such children are not capable of the sort of participation required, and secondly, because the exigencies of war demand rapid obedience to the commands of some clear-cut authority. Equally it would be ludicrous to attempt an authoritarian seminar for intelligent adults: first, because the adults are capable of the relevant participation, and secondly, because anything properly called a seminar could not (almost by definition) be conducted unless the participants actually participated on something like an egalitarian or democratic basis – if it was to be authoritarian it would simply turn into a situation where the professor dictated to the students what they should think and say.

We can see that little or nothing is gained by doctrinaire preferences (authoritarian, democratic, etc.). The fact is that very often we do not know what regimes really suit what sorts of people when they conduct various kinds of business. One difficulty is that people may think that a particular regime suits them – usually one in which they are given more direct power in decision-making –

but be wrong. Not only may the regime be inefficient for conducting whatever particular business they are engaged in, but it may also make them feel unhappy, insecure and desperately anxious. Whether it really suits all societies to have a democratic government or teenagers to have complete control over their own sexual behaviour are questions that need more psychological and sociological knowledge, although, of course, climates of feeling usually foreclose the questions in different ways at different times.

For what suits their own clientele, teachers can only rely on their common sense and experience, assisted by whatever psychologists and others can tell us. But we can make a good deal more progress by being clear about what suits the business we are conducting. For thereby we become clear about what sorts of decisions need to be made and what sorts of authorities we need to accept and obey: what rules and sanctions are necessary for the business, and what considerations are relevant and irrelevant. Where the nature of our business is fairly obvious, we usually manage to do this: nobody would think of running an army by democratic vote, or trying to solve a mathematical problem by deferring to the Führer or the Chief Constable. It is when we are less clear about what we are trying to do that we have doubts about the nature of the authority needed.

If education is to do with the planning of serious and sustained learning, then we have at least a few obvious points to bear in mind. First, authority must be exercised to ensure that such learning can in fact take place, and to encourage it. By the same token, we do not require authority to go beyond the purposes of learning. Thus, at least prima facie, the authority would have power and scope to ensure that the pupils did a minimum of work, turned up on time, did not disrupt the teaching, did not interfere with each other in such a way as to prevent each other from learning, and so on. Equally, it would *not* have the power or scope to dictate, say, the pupils' dress or hairstyles, unless it could be shown that these directly affected their learning. Of course this is only a very general point: a great deal will depend on *what* is to be learned and – something that follows from that – the *contexts* in which it can best be learned. Both these may be disputed. But at some stage we shall have to commit ourselves (and our pupils) to some sort of content, some set of objectives, and the important thing is to spell these out as clearly as we can. The question of authority can only be answered in that light.

Secondly, we can ensure that the authority (together with the rules and sanctions that go with it) is *clearly defined* in its scope and powers, and *properly enforced*. These are, again, obvious points, if much neglected in practice. Everyone in the business – ourselves, the pupils, their parents and all those connected with the enterprise – needs to know what the rules are, and what sanctions back them up: who can enforce what upon whom, by what methods and under what circumstances. Unless this is done, those in the business will not know where they are, and if the situation is too vague, the whole existence of any authority may be called into question, with the result that what actually happens is determined by pressure groups, vociferous individuals, power-seekers or mere inertia. It is from this sort of chaos, in which the strongest has his or her way and the weakest goes to the wall, that the entire apparatus of authority, rules, laws, constitutions, sanctions and the rest is supposed to save us; and unless it is defended with remorseless clarity, as well as being revised and overhauled when necessary, chaos is the inevitable result.

Thirdly, we can try (by whatever methods seem appropriate) to show our pupils that the ideal form of authority – for serious learners – really consists of the rules, procedures and standards inherent in what is being learned. Teachers and other educators act as mediators between these standards and the pupils. Their job is to bring the pupils, as far as possible, to a state in which they are willing and able to pursue the subjects for their own sake – that is, to obey the demands of truth that each subject incorporates. These demands, as any serious learner well knows, are no less stringent than the orders issued by teachers and other personalized authorities. It is again not a matter of escaping from authority and rules altogether, but of accepting the type of authority and rules that is most nearly appropriate to the activity. The whole point of the teacher's authority is to move pupils in this direction.

Finally, there is the much more difficult question of the legitimacy of authority in education. Assume that the pupils ought to learn what we want them to learn, that we set up a system of authority in schools that is more or less correct in scope, form, clarity and enforcement, that we encourage the pupils to question and learn about authority in appropriate ways, and that we succeed in making serious learners of them. Even then, it might be asked, by what right do we *compel* them to undergo this process, however desirable it may be? Who are the 'we' that assume the right to enforce this? Do not the pupils themselves have some say in the matter?

The traditional arguments advanced to justify this compulsion include the idea that the desirability of education is alone sufficient, that pupils are too young or too inexperienced to know what their best interests are, and that, being in this state, they can fairly be regarded as under orders (as well as under protection) emanating from their parents, or the state, or some other people to whom authority is delegated – including teachers. In default of lengthy discussion we must frankly say that these arguments seem entirely unsatisfactory, particularly when applied to (for example) an intelligent 15-year-old who does not wish to remain at school but who is legally compelled to do so. At the least, it seems hardly consistent to apply compulsion to such pupils 'in their own best interests' when we do not apply it to others to whom these same arguments might apply – for instance, to the senile, to the hopelessly neurotic, to developing nations, and so on.

As far as is possible – and of course with young children it is not possible – we ought surely to adopt the standard liberal practice of negotiation rather than imposition. Roughly speaking, what happens is that the child waives his or her rights and freedom as an individual in return for protection and nurture: he or she can at least be construed as giving the parents (society, teachers, etc.) a kind of mandate. Only such a basis would justify such imposition – that is, only if we can construe the pupils as voluntarily or contractually putting themselves in the hands of the educator, much as a sick person may put him or herself in the hands of the doctor and surgeon, who may then justifiably command him or her.

Although this is not, in fact, the legal position, the notion of a contract has important practical applications for teachers. First, it can reasonably be represented to the pupils that, if there *was* a chance for them to make a free contract, they would be well advised to contract for at least some education. Quite a lot of serious learning is required if they are to survive in society, and a good deal more if they are to pull their weight – something that society usually demands if it is going to protect them and offer them its services. Secondly, even if they would not freely accept a large part of education, they have nevertheless to adopt some clearly defined attitude to the system as it stands: either to accept (however grudgingly) or to reject. Teachers and pupils are here in the same boat. It is not the teacher's fault that this compulsion is applied (and teachers should exert whatever political power they have to produce a more rational situation). The teacher can say, in effect: 'This is the law, whether we like it or not. Given this – no doubt unreasonable – framework within which we have to operate, what kind of deal can we make with each other?'

The point is that, even when (perhaps particularly when) there is disagreement or resentment, we have to reach some sort of contractual agreement if we are to do any business together. The negotiation that this requires is often lengthy, arduous and discouraging; but it is better than a state of muddle and conflict in which both sides are, so to speak, trying to play quite different games on the same board. Agreement, however *ad hoc*, must be reached and the important thing is that those concerned should be *clearly committed* to it. Any method that will encourage such clear commitment – for instance, signing one's name to a set of rules – should be adopted. For without this commitment people (perhaps particularly the young) are apt to regard themselves as outside the game altogether, as able to obey rules when it suits them and disobey when it does not. But this is a parasitic attitude. Social expectations depend, as in the paradigm case of promise-keeping, on a commitment *in advance* to fulfil them.

Many more questions of this kind could, of course, be raised under the general heading 'authority', but we incline to think that practical answers can only be given by practising teachers – those who actually know the pupils and know what is both politically possible and educationally appropriate in each particular situation. There are many different kinds of schools, having very different relationships with the pupils' parents, local and central government, and the wider community, and pupils vary even more in various dimensions that may be relevant: age, sex, home background, intelligence and so on. It is no part of philosophy to lay down specific rules. Nor, in our judgement, have psychology and the social sciences advanced sufficiently to give the teacher much practical guidance. It must be left to his or her own common sense and imagination.

Nevertheless, there is a sort of general message (as we may call it) that we hope to have got across in the points made above. We are apt to think of authority as a kind of *object* or *force* that we possess in some quantity or other, rather as if we were wielding a stout or fragile stick. Some of us go on to wish that the stick were thicker, and others of us begin to feel guilty about wielding it at all. Even if we ourselves have grown out of these naive ideas, they are certainly present in our pupils' minds. What we have to do is to see clearly, and encourage our pupils to see, that authority is not like that at all, that it is more like the rules of a game or some other decision procedure that legitimizes and hence enables whatever business we are trying to do. Too many people still see rules, punishment and authority as restrictive and forbidding only, when in fact they are also enabling – just as keeping to the rules of a language, meaning what we say, may forbid us to use words wrongly, but is the only thing that enables us to communicate.

Given this sort of understanding, we have some hope of being able to sit down together to sort out what games we want to play. The practical difficulties that teachers face derive ultimately from our failure to do this, a failure that, admittedly, is not only or even chiefly the fault of teachers. A great many parties are involved: parents, local authorities, government, the state of the law and, of course, the pupils themselves. But it would be a good start if teachers were to be more insistent about reaching some clear agreement with these parties. One would hope that the agreement would entrust teachers with far more authority (and the power to go with it), since the complex business of education seems to demand this sort of set-up; but at least, whatever the agreement, all parties would know where they stood.

CHAPTER 2
Discipline and Power

If we are now clearer about authority, it will not be too hard to get clear about discipline and its relationship with power, provided, as always, we are prepared to shelve our particular feelings about these concepts and just *look at* them with an open mind. The questions to be asked here are of the form: 'Just what is discipline? What do we mean by "well-disciplined"? What concepts are we dealing with here?' Only when these are answered can we come to see what place discipline has in educational practice.

One broad or overall distinction at least must be enforced between whatever may be meant by pupils being well-disciplined on the one hand and various notions of the pupils being well-controlled, well-ordered, organized, or trouble-free on the other. Consider first the notion of a group of people or an institution being well-organized for a particular purpose. One can have a well-organized classroom, army, operating theatre or youth camp. This has to do with the arrangements, perhaps even more specifically with what one might call the administrative arrangements, that facilitate the purpose. A youth camp is badly organized if the latrines are too far away (or too near), an operating theatre if it is not arranged that the assistant with the scalpel stands near enough to the surgeon, and a classroom if the desks do not give the children a clear view of the board. To describe all this under the heading 'discipline' is palpably absurd. Now consider the notion of being trouble-free, or in a broad sense 'controlled'. We get trouble-free prisoners by putting them in chains, trouble-free children by slipping them tranquillizers, trouble-free surgical assistants, perhaps, by paying them enough for them not to worry about their mortgages during the operation. Again, this has nothing specifically to do with discipline. And we could run similar arguments with other notions applicable to groups of people, such as having high morale, enthusiasm, interested and so on.

'Accepting rules' is much nearer the target, because it brings in the notion of obedience. When we talk about the discipline of (say) an army being good, we are not talking about whether its administrative arrangements are good, or whether the soldiers are trouble-free and quiescent, or whether their morale and enthusiasm are high, although all these may, contingently, affect discipline or reflect it. We are talking about whether they obey the rules. Perhaps we mean something more than that, however: whether they can be relied on to obey the rules. Suppose we have soldiers who do obey the rules, but they do so rather slothfully and mutter curses under their breath and so on. That is better than if they did not obey them, and certainly they are better disciplined than soldiers who conduct wildly enthusiastic charges against the enemy on their own initiative. But we might think that their discipline was a bit suspect, about to crack or 'slack'. We are not concerned only with their overt obedience, but with some kind of disposition to obey.

Can we sharpen up the vagueness of 'some kind of disposition to obey'? First, of course, the well-disciplined soldier will not obey anyone – he will obey the established authority (his commanders or military regulations); naturally there can sometimes be a question about what or who is the established authority. More difficult, but crucial, is whether he must have certain reasons for his obedience. Granted that he obeys consistently and obeys the established authorities, does it matter why he obeys? He must, of course, obey for some kind of reason and in some degree of consciousness. If, for instance, he was just reacting to a set of post-hypnotic commands, that would not suffice to call him well-disciplined, and indeed we might wonder whether to allow this as a fully fledged case of obeying (it is rather more like animals obeying). But what kind of reasons must he use?

Suppose a Roman legion obeys Caesar consistently, but when Pompey takes it over the troops immediately grow slack and perhaps mutinous. We investigate and find that they obeyed Caesar because of his personal charm, not because he was the legitimate general; Pompey is also legitimate but charmless. Were they well-disciplined under Caesar? A science class is well-disciplined when in the hands of Mr X because they admire him and of Miss Y because they respect her, but disobedient with Mr Z because they hate him. Is the science class a well-disciplined class? Are they well-disciplined even with Mr X and Miss Y?

In a loose sort of way we call people 'well-disciplined' (or 'just' or 'kind', or all sorts of things) when their overt behaviour – as long as it has some sort of reason – is of a certain kind. But really the well-disciplined (just, kind, etc.) person has to have a particular type of reason. In the case of discipline, the point would be that the person must obey the rules because they are authoritative. This is importantly different from obeying them because they happen to issue from an admired source. It is also importantly different from obeying them because they are good rules, or sensible rules, or rules required for the purposes of the institution – a feature of rules constantly stressed in educational literature but irrelevant to the particular notion of discipline.

There is clearly a particular concept at stake here: roughly, the notion of *obedience to established and legitimate authorities as such*. One could say a very great deal about the practical importance of grasping this notion and making it part of one's life and behaviour. Indeed, it is difficult to see how, without this, any institution or society can do more than rely upon the *ad hoc* variety of bribes or threats that might get things done – Mr X's charm, Miss Y's obvious ability, payment for doing good homework, electric shocks, or anything else we may wish to deploy. But quite apart from any question of the inefficiency or fragility of such pressures, to omit the notion of discipline in this sense is to omit a whole swathe of concepts (authority, punishment, contract, law and so on) that are logically inevitable for rational creatures.

What is it to accept rules as 'authoritative'? What is it to obey something or somebody as a source of authority rather than just a source of power? We have somehow to tread a middle way between two ideas, neither of which co-extends with the idea of discipline, which we shall call 'total consent' and 'submission to power'. Some examples follow.

Roman soldiers were (sometimes) well-disciplined if anyone ever was. But it would be grotesque to say that they had always given anything like free or total consent to their authorities, or had in some way freely contracted to abide by the rules. Many of them had been automatically forced, conned, lured or press-ganged into service. Their good discipline plainly did not depend on a totally free acceptance, nor on their acceptance of the rules, commanders, campaigns, or anything else as necessarily good or desirable.

On the other hand, we cannot regard their behaviour – at those times when, and to the extent that, such behaviour was well-disciplined – as in any simple or direct way forced. They were not well-disciplined when their centurions had to cudgel them in order to get them to perform various tasks; my behaviour is not well-disciplined if I advance only because there is a sword at my back. Such behaviour may be in accordance with the rules in force, but my reason for so behaving is not to obey the rules. My thought is not 'I will advance, or else I shall have failed in my duty', but 'I will advance or else I shall get stabbed'.

To accept rules as authoritative, in the sense required for discipline, consists partly in accepting them as reasons for action. This is verified by whether, in the practical situations involved, the motivating thought is something like 'it's a rule', rather than, for example, 'it's a good idea', 'I shall suffer if I don't obey', 'I like doing this sort of thing', etc. Whether this is in fact what we have called the 'motivating thought' can, at least in principle, be established by setting up enough controlled situations in which the irrelevant variables do not apply. We see how the subject thinks and acts when it is a bad rule, when he or she will not suffer for disobedience, and so on.

Discipline is concerned with the consistency and strength of on-the-spot acceptances or cases of obedience to authority. This, of course, involves or presumes an overall acceptance of the authority as such, but it does not involve any question about why it is accepted. There may be all kinds of reasons why a person accepts or submits to a source of power. We may do this in something like total freedom, as perhaps when we decide to learn French and put ourselves in the hands of a French teacher. Or, more commonly, we may think that the existing political authorities, rotten though they are, represent the only practically desirable alternative at the present time, and so consent to their rules. Or we may simply find ourselves (perhaps more commonly still) in a situation where we have no immediate means of escape from the authorities or powers-that-be and opt to 'play their game', either because it is the best we can do for ourselves or because of mere inertia. Many other possibilities exist. The analogy with games, weak at some points, is here strong: why a person plays in the first place (and his or her general outlook on the game as a whole) is one thing; his or her detailed obedience to the rules is another.

Of course not all these rules are of the same kind, or stem from the same authority. A lot here turns on the subject of whom 'well-disciplined' is predicated. Thus we conceive of a soldier, for the most part, as one who obeys the orders of others, these orders being represented in a fairly concrete form. That is, as long as he does what his superiors tell him, and obeys regulations laid down in some manual or rule-book, he is well-disciplined. It is not required that he should, on his own initiative, improve his marksmanship or map-reading – that (for a soldier) shows him to be keener or more dedicated, but not better disciplined. A soldier's disciplinary duty begins and ends with obedience to others. A well-disciplined chess player, athlete or fencer, on the other hand, obeys rules inherent in his or her craft; such people are not just occupiers of roles, but also craftsmen. The chess player restrains his eagerness in deference to principles concerned with building up an adequate defence before attacking, the athlete paces herself rather than just running flat out, and so on.

Pace the Latin derivation of the word 'discipline', it is today a little odd to use 'well-disciplined' even in such cases, just as it is odd to talk of someone as 'well-disciplined' in his or her moral relationships with other people. Perhaps this is because 'discipline' is most at home when closely connected with fairly clear-cut social rules and situations: in an army, in an operating theatre, in a classroom, on a ship. The demands we make under 'discipline' seem pretty down-to-earth. Thus we may say of a citizen who pays taxes, keeps the peace, etc., that he is law-abiding, but not that he is well-disciplined. Now put him in ancient Sparta, where his life is much more a matter of quasi-military obligation, and the word becomes more natural. Most natural of all is its use not of an individual, but of a group: it is not, or certainly not primarily, Smith minor or Private Jones or Amompharetus who are well-disciplined, but the Lower Fifth, the Second Battalion and the Spartan army. Individuals are more likely to be described as simply 'disobedient'.

This does not imply, of course, anything about the constitutional basis (as one might call it) of the group. Roles, tasks and duties may be allotted democratically – that is, as a result of discussion and majority vote – or by a dictator. Discipline prevails when these duties are carried out in obedience to the rules. Constitutional questions about who makes the rules, what methods there are of changing them, etc., are here irrelevant. It is perhaps a contingent fact that social groups who operate democratically create fewer contexts in which it is appropriate to speak of 'discipline' than do less democratic groups – that is, fewer contexts in which there are those more or less quasi-military obligations that make the word natural. For example, a ship's company with a democratic constitution, within which everyone participated in decision-making, would in practice be more suited to a pleasure cruise than a battle; and we would not speak so easily of 'discipline' on a pleasure cruise. But it would be possible for a ship or a fleet to change its constitution in the direction of democracy, at least to some degree, and still to operate in contexts where discipline is relevant – that is, by continuing to allot rules and tasks in a military style.

We can go further on these lines with the notion of 'task' and 'authority'. For 'discipline', 'well-disciplined', etc., to be in place, the task has to be a fairly specific or practical one. It is not a matter of discipline whether Christians obey the authority of priest or scriptures in such matters as forgiving their enemies, loving their neighbours, and so on; on the other hand, it is so if monks obey or disobey more specific instructions, emanating from the abbot or the rules of their order. Similarly, revolutionaries might be praised for ordering their lives according to the precepts of, say, Marx; but they would only be praised for being well-disciplined in so far as they obeyed the orders of the revolutionary leader or committee. Being, in general, a good Christian or a good Marxist is not a task in the required sense.

Equally, the task must be specific to the authority and the group – not just any obedience to accepted authority will do. A local policeman may often issue commands to the citizens in his neighbourhood, but the citizens' obedience is not a case of good discipline in the way that the obedience of the policeman's subordinates in the police force would be. The citizens are under the policeman's authority but not, one might say, under his discipline. So too a teacher as an adult may give orders to children, but whether or not such orders can be regarded as authoritative, obedience to them is only a matter of discipline if the children are a working group under her particular authority for a particular purpose – if, that is, she gives her orders as the teacher of a particular class of pupils or at least as a teacher in the school of which they are members.

Obviously a group can be well-disciplined in respect of one

authority and badly disciplined in respect of another -- for instance, the members of a revolutionary organization. Similarly, pupils' behaviour may be guided by the authority of their peer group or gang, or even perhaps of the school bully, rather than that of the teacher. We might have difficulty in deciding whether we could sensibly talk of authority here, rather than just power or influence. Clearly, authority requires something in the way of formal recognition or acceptance (legitimization) and has to be to some degree institutionalized. But it is plain that two or more potential authorities might compete for obedience, even within the fairly narrow sphere demarcated by discipline.

Finally, there will be some occasions on which we might hesitate to use well-disciplined or badly-disciplined at all, not because the kind of task or authority is logically inappropriate but more simply because obedience is either non-existent or so negligible that the terms are out of place. The notion of discipline involves some presumption that the group is meant to be, and is minimally trying to be, obedient: this involves some expectation of obedience. A continuing total lack of such obedience would extinguish such expectation. If pupils constantly paid no serious attention to the teacher at all, we should not say that they were badly disciplined or even that the discipline was appalling – we should say that there was no discipline at all.

We ought now to have gained something that is of particular relevance to the practical teacher – that is, an idea of discipline as an educational objective in its own right and not just as a facilitator for education. One might perhaps categorize it under moral or political education. It involves the understanding and practice of a particular virtue, confined to particular types of situation that are nevertheless of great practical importance: roughly situations that are 'tight' enough for us to want to speak of discipline as against more general terms, such as law-abiding. This has very little to do with notions vaguely canvassed under such headings as autonomy, self-discipline and others, and has to be sharply separated from them.

There are reasons why this particular educational objective is important, and why it is currently in dispute. Briefly, it will appear to liberally minded adults in a civilized, peaceful and pluralistic society as if the number of tightly structured, quasi-military situations in which our pupils are likely to find themselves is small, and as if such situations are either not very important or positively objectionable (perhaps as leading to conformism, authoritarianism, or whatever). Conversely there are those who are naturally predisposed to such situations, and who will instinctively favour increasing them (one thinks here of demands to reintroduce military service, perhaps of Outward Bound courses, and so on). Leaving prejudice aside, however, we need to note the following points.

1. It is inevitable that children are born and will spend some years in a situation that is tightly structured in the way described. The family is a group of this kind – so are the classroom and the school as a whole. Notions like obedience, duties, allotted tasks, and so on, are here essential. If a child did not grasp and act upon the principle of discipline, of obedience to established authority, he or she could hardly survive at all, and a proper grasp of this is an essential enablement for the child to learn other things.

2. Because of this, discipline – although *per se* it is only one sub-heading of the general area of contractual obligation, acting out of principle, rule-following and so forth – is inevitably a crucially important area. The family and the school necessarily form the arena of the child's first encounter with the whole business of rules and authority. If she does not grasp the relevant points in this arena, it is unlikely (certain developmentalists might say impossible) that she will do so later when she comes to wider and less structured contexts in which the word 'discipline' is less applicable.

3. Although not many social groups are 'military', a great many are more like a peace-time army than they are like (say) a university or a collection of bohemian artists. We may legitimately speak of 'discipline' in groups of people building bridges, making cars, digging coal, trawling for fish, and in a large number of other cases. It is clear enough that, no matter how 'liberal' our or any other society may be, we should not survive very long without adequate discipline in such contexts. And these are the contexts in which most of our pupils will in fact operate.

The contrast between discipline, in the sense outlined, and the quite different notion of being 'controlled' or 'trouble-free', is one that teachers (whether they know it or not) face every day. Not infrequently it produces a conflict of aims. Given sufficient charm, bribes, rewards, etc. or just the willingness to overlook offences, it may be possible to keep a class of pupils trouble-free. If we insist on discipline, we may create more trouble rather than less (just as, in some industrial situations, it pays the management to 'square' their workers by any means possible, without worrying about contractual obligations or fair play or anything of that kind; or just as, if you wished to survive as a Roman emperor, you gave donatives to the troops, regardless of whether they deserved it). Many teachers are in a position where they are doing well if they can survive – it seems a bit much to ask them to take on discipline as well. If they let offenders get away with it, who shall blame them? Bribe the bully, let the tiresome child play truant, put the badly behaved out of the room if absolutely necessary, overlook the rule-breaker, turn a blind eye to the lazy and thank God for the end of term.

It is sometimes said that good discipline has no necessary connections with the *power* wielded by teachers. After all, teachers have sometimes had plenty of power (including power to deploy savage forms of corporal punishment, as in the nineteenth-century public schools) but nevertheless discipline was very bad. Hence, we might think, it is not so much power but *authority* that matters – that is, the acceptance by the clients that X has the *right* to obedience (not just the strength to enforce it). If it were just a matter of power, the motivating thought in the client's head would be, 'I had better obey, or else I shall get clobbered', and that, as we have seen, is not the thought characteristic of good discipline. The correct thought is 'because the *authority* says so'. Hence (the story might go) we need not worry about whether teachers have enough powers; we need only worry about whether their authority is sufficient, about whether they are recognized as having the right to give orders and lay down rules.

There is a basic objection to this, which may be put either philosophically or empirically. Empirically, it is a fairly safe bet that if some authority lacks the power to make its orders and rules stick – the power to enforce obedience – it will rapidly cease to be seen as an authority. At most, it will be an authority *de jure* and not *de facto*. The client might say: 'Well, I suppose that ideally so-and-so ought' (one might put 'ought' in inverted commas here) 'to be obeyed. After all he is legally in charge. But in fact I shall obey someone else who actually has the power, or just act to suit myself.'

With the passage of time the *de jure* authority becomes more and more academic, more and more a matter of some moral judgement abstracted from the real world; perhaps there is some sense in which descendants of the Tsar have the right to rule in Russia, but in fact the authority is now vested in others. Philosophically, and in one way more severely, we might rely on an earlier argument and say that social authorities (not other kinds of 'experts') must by definition be able to issue *rules*, and that unless rules are characteristically backed by enforcement and disadvantaging they are no longer rules. If the authorities do not have the power to make the rules stick, they have become advisers or representatives of ideals rather than authorities. There is, in fact, a (loose) conceptual connection between authority (in this sense) and power.

The argument shows only, though importantly, that power is not a *sufficient* condition for discipline (since it does not generate the correct motivating thought). Certainly, it is a necessary condition. Even with mature adults, the law would not be the law (but only a set of pious hopes or ideals) unless it were ultimately backed by some kind of force or power, not because people will only obey the law through fear of punishment – they might have many more high-minded reasons for obedience – but because there must be some back-up to ensure obedience when these high-minded reasons fail. *A fortiori*, children, particularly young children, may come to recognize and accept the authority of teachers and parents without the constant need for demonstrations of power; but if that power were not there as a background they would not be so accepting of an *authority*.

CHAPTER 3
Rules and Contracts

The third area we need to be clear about is the area of rules and contracts, which is of course closely connected with the other concepts – authority, discipline and punishment. This is not easy, because we, as well as our pupils, tend often to misunderstand the area and lapse into postures that may be labelled 'authoritarian', 'liberal', 'progressive', 'Victorian', etc., all of which are partly the result of muddle and prejudice.

The first point is that rules and authorities in a school, or any other institution, or in society generally, are not to be regarded as ends in themselves. They are not there by divine right, so to speak, or because the authorities are powerful and can make people obey. For it must always be possible to question the rules or the authorities, to think about whether they are right or wrong. To put it another way: getting people to think, to make up their own minds reasonably, comes first, and the function of rules and authorities must be subordinated to this end.

Very roughly, this is the underlying assumption of a liberal society as opposed to a totalitarian or dictatorial one. People sometimes think that a liberal society means one in which you can do as you like, whereas in a totalitarian society you do what you are told. In fact, all societies have rules and authorities. The real difference is in what the function of the rules and authorities is supposed to be. In liberal societies the function is partly to give people freedom and security so that they can think for themselves; in totalitarian ones the rules and authorities make up the individuals' minds for them – they are not supposed to think or question, just to obey the rules or be indoctrinated into whatever the authorities think is best for them. What we object to in totalitarian societies, like Nazi Germany, is not just that they had bad rules and bad authorities: much more important is that they felt they had the right to tell people what to think. They used rules and authorities to produce the sort of people with the sort of beliefs they wanted.

Once we understand this, another thing becomes obvious, and that is that what rules and authorities you have is just as important for liberal societies as for totalitarian ones. You cannot help people to think, or educate them, or bring them up to be free and reasonable, just by leaving them alone and having no rules at all. People sometimes talk as if anything you could call a 'rule' must somehow be a wicked thing imposed by some tyrannical authority. But in fact without following rules we would not be human beings at all. Rules are needed to play games, do business, drive cars, arrange for people to be fed and housed, and for every other human activity. You cannot think or talk without following rules, the rules of language.

Every child, and every adult too, needs a framework and a set of rules. It is not just that he or she feels more secure in such a framework, although (particularly for young children) that is also true; it is rather that, without such a framework, he or she will never learn anything. For instance, if we want to teach something to two children in a primary school, we cannot even begin to do this if they are fighting, or not listening, or drunk, or suffering terribly from toothache. We have to arrange for certain *preconditions* for educating people to be established: in particular, we have to arrange things so that they can communicate with each other and learn from other people.

This is very much like the rules needed to make the methods of even the most liberal society work at all. A primitive society might settle its disputes by fighting, so that the strongest party wins. Then perhaps we make progress, and agree to talk things over by means of a discussion or a parliamentary debate. But this at once means that we have to have rules: you cannot have a discussion or a debate if people are throwing spears at each other. Indeed the rules you need to follow in order to get a good discussion or debate are quite complicated. It does not work well if people insult or shout at each other, or keep interrupting. You need rules of procedure. You also, of course, have to make sure that people are not too ill or upset to discuss things, that they are adequately defended against any external enemies, that they have had enough to eat, and so on.

We have to remember, then, that rules are supposed to have *point* or *purpose*: to make a better game, to get a proper discussion, or whatever. Of course, some rules may not have much point, and can be scrapped; other rules may be very important and well-suited to what we are trying to do; others again may need some improvement or additions. It all depends on what we are trying to achieve. We have to have one kind of rule for a company of soldiers in battle, another for a cricket team and another for a classroom discussion or a parliamentary debate. None of these have to be 'moral' rules, if by that we mean that we look on them as ideally right or good in themselves. It is just that they serve particular human needs, wants or interests.

This is why both the notion of total conformity and the notion of total anarchy are logically absurd for human beings. For if people always obeyed the rules, never questioning them, but simply going through the patterns of behaviour that the rules prescribed, we would not be able to distinguish them from animals governed entirely by their instincts, like birds building nests, or ants or bees. It is part of the concept of a human being that she is capable of not conforming – that if she follows rules, then to some extent she does so deliberately and of her own free will. But equally, and for similar reasons, anarchy is impossible for human beings. For humans learn to talk and think by conforming to the rules governing language and meaning. And apart from this basic consideration, anything that we could properly call a society would involve a number of human beings making some kinds of contracts with each other – and contracts are a form of rule-keeping. Those who call themselves anarchists are usually protesting (whether they know it or not) against *particular* authorities or *particular* kinds of rules, not against having any rules at all.

All this means that what sort of rules we ought to have, in particular contexts and for particular purposes, is a very open question, which can often only be settled by finding out more facts than we know already. For instance, it is pretty obvious that for many (perhaps all) purposes we need to have rules about telling the truth, keeping promises, and not hurting or killing people. It would be hard to see how any communal activity could flourish if we did not, for the most part, abide by such rules: although of course we may make exceptions in special cases. But there will be plenty of other cases where we are not sure whether we need rules in a certain area or not, or are not sure about what rules to have.

We might agree that for the purposes of having an efficient army we had to subject the soldiers to certain disciplinary regulations. Obviously one rule must be that they obey their officers. But what about making them keep their uniforms clean, and drill on the parade ground? Some would argue that this is a waste of time, and that their efficiency as a fighting force would not be impaired – or might even be improved – if there were no rules in this area. Others might claim that cleanliness of uniform and drill contribute to efficiency. In fact, of course, we cannot be sure of the answer to this – we might have to rely on guesswork and the collective experience of army officers. But we would try to settle the question, not by saying that soldiers *just ought* to conform to these rules, nor by saying that the rules were just silly traditions or conventions that ought to be scrapped at once. We would settle the question on the evidence, and try to find out whether or not such rules contributed to the purposes we wished to achieve.

Again, we might agree that at a university or college the purpose of having students there was so that they might learn certain subjects efficiently – so it would obviously be necessary to have rules of some kind or other to ensure that they worked reasonably hard, read the right books, turned up for lectures, or whatever was thought essential to the purpose of learning. But what about rules governing their 'private lives', such as rules about sexual behaviour or dress? Here too we must not be doctrinaire: we must not say, with unthinking conformity, that they just ought to keep certain rules because this produces 'decent behaviour' or 'proper manners'; but nor must we say, with an over-hasty rebelliousness, that the rules are certainly irrelevant to the purpose. It might be the case that certain types of sexual behaviour affect the student's ability to learn – for good or ill – or it might be the case that they make no difference.

Young children are not, in general, capable of making up their own rules in a sensible way. Indeed, they are not capable of understanding the kind of considerations mentioned above. They would not be able to understand them unless we made them follow certain rules in the first place, for only in this way can they come to grasp the whole idea of rules and the purpose of rules. So in effect parents and teachers *initiate* children into certain contexts that are governed by rules, in the hope that when they are older and have learnt more about the world they will be able to make up their own minds in a reasonable way. We give children more and more freedom as they get older, until when they are adult we allow them to choose their own way of life for themselves.

Naturally there are difficulties about the particular point at which it seems right to consider children as 'grown up'. In general, we feel that we have some kind of mandate or right to supervise young children. We do not regard them as completely free and responsible agents, so we curtail their liberty, and in return we look after them – feed, house, clothe and protect them, give them education and guidance, and so on. At some time – perhaps at the school-leaving age, when they can be economically independent if they wish – we give up this mandate. Thereafter we hope that they may wish to continue being educated, and will want to learn from other people in our society, but we cannot enforce this. This is the position that applies, in some degree at least, to sixth-formers and university and college students.

But when the child or adolescent is considered to be adult, and has become free of the particular rules that were imposed by parents and teachers, he or she does not thereby become free of all rules. It is in principle possible that an adult could live entirely alone on a desert island, owing nothing to and being owed nothing by any other person, but even this is in practice impossible (all desert islands belong to somebody nowadays). In fact he or she will go to college, or do a job, or at any rate exist as a member of some sovereign state – the United Kingdom, or France, or somewhere else. Unlike the young child, the adult can opt for one out of a number of possibilities: he does not *have* to go to college, if she dislikes Britain she can emigrate, and so on. But the adult will certainly be within one rule-governed situation or another.

In effect, the adult enters more or less consciously and deliberately into some kind of *contract*. This may not be an obvious and ordinary contract, such as that between a worker and an employer, or one trader and another, but it will be a contract just the same. It is helpful here to think of choosing a contract in the light of choosing whether to play a particular game. By choosing to play cricket, bridge or anything else, one contracts to obey a particular set of rules in common with other people. Often the rules do not cover every possible contingency, so that there are authorities empowered to interpret them, such as umpires in cricket and referees in football.

Part of the contract is that the players are supposed to accept the umpire's or referee's ruling – the officials are, so to speak, part of the rules of the game. In just the same way, in any society, there will be rules (sometimes in the form of constitutions) and authorities: parliaments, vice-chancellors, headteachers, school committees and so forth.

Of course these contracts work both ways. The contractor not only is obliged to obey the rules, but also is entitled to receive benefits under the rules. For instance, part of the contract in this country is that citizens pay income tax, the money from which is spent on things like roads, education, a health service and so on, which are of use to those citizens. At a university, students agree to obey the rules about lectures, reading books, etc., and receive in return the teaching and opportunities for learning that the university provides. In the army, soldiers accept military law, in return for which the army clothes, feeds and in general looks after the soldiers.

However, as we have seen, rules and contracts that embody rules can be changed. In order to make a change, we need some kind of *decision procedure*; that is, some kind of agreement about legitimate and illegitimate ways of changing the rules. Thus if we were forming a social club, or a small society on a desert island, we would probably think something like: 'Well, let's have such-and-such rules for the time being, since these seem the most sensible ones. But maybe we shall want to change them in the future. Now what shall we do – shall we elect a boss who can change the rules at any time, or a small committee of three people who can change them? Or shall we say that everybody must vote, and that the rules can only be changed if more than 50 per cent are in favour? Or should we require two-thirds in favour? Or what?' In coming thus to agree about what ways of changing the rules we *were* going to allow, we should also be agreeing about what ways we were *not* going to allow. For instance, we would probably say, 'We'll discuss changes in the rules, but people mustn't keep shouting or fighting during the discussions. We will allow people to make speeches, or carry banners with slogans, but we won't allow them to throw bricks or spears', and so on.

Here we have not just the ordinary rules, but rules about changing rules, rules about decision procedures. In any large society this usually means some agreement about the 'sovereign body', the ultimate court of appeal. In the UK Parliament is normally taken to be sovereign, but in other countries it might be a particular oligarchy, a dictator or the will of the people as expressed in a vote or referendum. There will also be rules, more or less clearly stated, about what is allowable by way of trying to change the rules: putting pressure on a Member of Parliament, peaceful demonstration and speaking in Hyde Park are all legitimate; throwing bombs or assassinating prime ministers is not.

All this is going to apply to any society, to any contractual situation or 'game' played in common, even to a small society of two members, such as a married couple. We may hope, of course, that it will not be necessary to spell out all the rules all the time. In marriage, for instance, the couple may get on together so well that they need not bother to keep thinking about their contractual obligations or decision procedures. On the other hand, if there is any trouble or difficulty, we are inevitably thrown back on some such agreement. The only alternative to such agreement is for a person to opt out of that particular society altogether.

It is not likely that we shall be able to offer every individual exactly the sort of 'game' or contract that he or she likes. We might prefer to have the rules of cricket changed, so that we are not obliged to spend long and boring hours fielding rather than batting; but if we cannot get them changed, then either we must play cricket and put up with having to field, or else we cannot play cricket. Similarly, in any contract or society, there will probably be things that we dislike, or of which we morally disapprove, or that we regard as irrational, tiresome, silly, scandalous or wicked. Naturally we shall try to get these changed, but if we want to join the society at all then we are obliged to keep the rules in the meantime and we are obliged to restrict ourselves to allowable methods of getting the rules changed, since the rules about what methods are allowable are themselves among the rules we contract for.

If you are born and brought up in Britain, you are faced with a choice. By remaining part of the system, you get whatever advantages the system has – such things as a health service, social security if you are out of work, free education, law and order, and so forth. You also have the right to try to change any rules you disapprove of by certain methods. On the other hand, you have to keep the rules that permit these advantages – paying income tax, not stealing, etc. – and the rules that disallow certain methods of change, such as using violence on other people or setting fire to buildings. Thus you are not obliged to believe that all the rules are particularly good rules, or that the values enshrined in British society are the right ones, but you are obliged to play the game according to the rules if you wish to stay in this society. You can either accept this contractual obligation if you think it is worth your while, or you can refuse and emigrate, or live outside society in some other way, such as by breaking the law.

All this would remain true in any situation or society. But this is not to say that the rules in any particular society are good ones. We may think that the rules about decision procedures and the general structures of many societies are very unsatisfactory in that they do not allow enough people to participate in making decisions enough of the time. Situations develop in which society gets divided into 'we', who are on the receiving end of the rules, and 'they', who make the rules. Workers, students and others feel that the rules are not *their* rules. Of course, even if they are not, these people still have to decide whether to contract for them or opt out of society altogether. But it is quite understandable that they feel left out of the most important part of the game; that is, left out of making and changing the rules. There is a lot to be said about how to make societies more democratic, bring more people into the game and hence avoid these difficulties, and it is very important that particular societies – not only countries such as the UK, but also smaller societies like universities and schools – should devote a good deal of thought to this.

When such difficulties arise, a lot of trouble is caused by *lack of clarity about the contract*. For instance, to take a topical case, the university authorities may have a very vaguely stated expectation that the students will 'behave reasonably' or 'not bring the university into disrepute'. But this might be interpreted quite differently, in practice, by the authorities and the students. If what was meant by 'behaving reasonably' was clearly spelled out, and the students were asked either to contract for this or not to come to the university, we could avoid trouble. This is true of other situations. Trouble arises partly because it is *not clear what the rules are*. If everyone shares common values and ways of behaving, this does not matter much; but we live in a time when this is not so, and the only thing is to get both parties to state clearly what rules they want to contract for.

This is something that students, workers and others who often feel that rules are just authoritarian impositions can try to achieve. Too often we see authorities trying simply to maintain their authority without clarity about rules and without clear justifications of the rules, and those under the authority's control simply rebelling in an aimlessly aggressive way, dissatisfied with the system but without any clear views about what changes are required. There are vested interests on both sides: the authorities may mask theirs by talking about law and order, decent behaviour and so on; and the underdogs may deceive themselves that they are acting out of idealism, reformist zeal, etc.

This applies, of course, not only to the contracts in society (e.g. the UK) or in institutions (e.g. a university), but also to contracts in particular social contexts. To take a topical example: if somebody comes to speak at a meeting, he or she will want to know what the rules of the meeting are to be. Here there are various possibilities: one may have rules that allow heckling, as seems to be the case in some political assemblies, or rules that allow demonstrations, making it impossible for the speaker to speak, or rules that allow throwing eggs (in which case the speaker may bring eggs of his or her own), or almost anything. What matters is that the rules are specified beforehand, and enforced. Again, either we can have a football match in which the players just play football without interference, or we can allow a situation in which police, casual spectators, demonstrators and others prevent any football being played at all; or, if we really want it, we can have a sort of mob scene in which football may be played (if the police win) or may not (if the demonstrators win). Any of these rule-governed systems or 'games' can be specified in advance.

Naturally various people will have a vested interest in *not* having the rules clearly specified. These may be the authorities, who keep the rules deliberately vague in order (perhaps) to be able to clamp down on any particular piece of behaviour which in their opinion, or 'public opinion', or the opinions of a certain social class, is distasteful or disruptive. (Laws and law-enforcement about obscenity, censorship and sexual matters generally seem to be of this kind.) Or they may be minority groups who wish to take advantage of unclear rule-systems in order to make their will felt. Anyone who has ever found himself in an authority role will readily appreciate the temptation to leave things unspecified, to 'smudge it', 'let sleeping dogs lie', etc.; and anyone who has ever found herself in a minority group that feels passionately about some cause or other will readily understand how such groups may benefit from lack of contractual clarity. But it will not do. Some contractual system must be logically and morally prior to any particular moves we may make to advance particular causes or beliefs.

This is not to say, of course, that it is desirable (or even possible) for us to formulate in advance rules to cover *every* contingency. We may well think it better, in many cases, to empower some authority to decide *ad hoc* on what is permissible and what is not. In any case we shall need an authority (judge, umpire, etc.) to interpret the rules. But this too can be made absolutely clear. Thus, if we know that there are *some* clear rules governing our behaviour as teachers, but that otherwise our behaviour will be accepted or objected to, rewarded or punished, at the discretion of the headteacher, then at least we know where we are: we can study the headteacher and act accordingly. Again, if we want a set-up in which the police can punish behaviour in the area of sex and obscenity more or less at will, or under the cover of extremely vague laws, then (regrettable though this may be) at least we must be honest and proclaim that this *is* the set-up. How much latitude should be given to authorities is a question that can only be answered by considering each case on its own merits. What is important is that the answer in each case should be clearly specified.

It will be worth our while here to take a look at some common but misguided alternatives to the contract system. They can for our purposes be lumped together, because they all attempt to substitute some first-order consensus for the second-order principle of con-tractual agreement. This first-order consensus is not often spelled out in detail, in the form of specific moral judgements about pre-cisely what clothes should be worn, what exact types of sexual behaviour are good and bad, etc. More commonly reference is made to what is reasonable, what most right-minded people would accept, decent behaviour, and so forth. In one form or another, this is perhaps the most popular approach in almost all societies to specific problems of misconduct. It is a kind of modern-dress version of saying 'it's just not *done*', with the implication that no 'right-minded' (decent, reasonable, etc.) person would do it.

As long as such a consensus actually exists widely and strongly enough, then of course sufficient uniformity of behaviour and social expectations can be achieved. But it hardly needs pointing out that, in most industrialized societies today, it does not exist. If it did, the problems that we are trying to cope with would not exist either. As long, for instance, as Oxbridge or other students shared a common intuitive perception about what counted as 'gentlemanly behaviour', or what could be said to 'bring the university into disrepute', and as long as this intuitive perception carried enough weight for them to determine their conduct by it, then there simply could not *be* demonstrations, slogans painted on college walls, or cricket pitches destroyed in the name of racial integration. As long as sixth-formers and other adolescents accepted the code of behaviour expected of them by teachers and other adults, they were part of the consensus and would not (almost by definition) act against it.

This sort of consensus does not have to be spelled out in detail, because it relies on the acceptance of a kind of authority. Certain people – parents, teachers, dons, or 'public opinion' as evidenced by friends and neighbours – are regarded as the touchstones or arbiters for determining the content of the consensus in each case. Thus a schoolboy or student who was uncertain about whether it was 'acceptable' or 'decent' not to wear a tie on some occasion, or to kiss his girl friend in public, would try to settle the question by asking himself what his schoolteacher or tutor would think about it. The breakdown in the consensus in our times has been dramatic precisely because these authorities or arbiters are no longer accepted as such by many people. It is not so much that such people disagree about this or that specific application of the consensus, but rather that the whole consensus has fallen into disregard because the adults who back it and instantiate it have fallen into disregard as authorities. When this happens, the game is wide open, for the defining rules are no longer accepted: it is not a question of replacing one rule within the game by another preferred rule, but rather of rejecting the whole game.

It is fatal (and fatally common) either to pretend that the consensus exists when it does not, or to attempt a new consensus of the same kind. This is a classic error committed by nearly all those in some position of authority, whether as governments, vice-chancellors, headteachers or whatever. What happens is something like this. First, the authorities will pretend or even believe that there is no problem: 'really' the consensus still exists, it is just a few unruly students or drunken rioters who cause the trouble and the majority of right-thinking citizens still have a clear idea of what is good and bad. Then, if trouble nevertheless persists, the authorities will make certain fashionable concessions: perhaps they now allow demonstrations in the streets provided they are not *too* violent, or they let students stay out until 2 a.m. instead of 10 p.m., or they no longer insist that sixth-formers wear school uniform. By such measures they seem to themselves to be modern, progressive, in keeping with the times, etc., and avoid the image of Victorian sternness. Nowadays we are all to some degree 'permissive'.

What is boring and dangerous about this is that it fails to meet the problem at all. *Ad hoc* measures of this sort represent nothing more than a vague desire to be fashionable, and a hand-to-mouth attempt to keep trouble down to a minimum – to keep the students and adolescents, the trades unionists, the potential trouble-makers of whatever kind, *in play*, and to avoid an explosion. The implication is that the authorities are still posing as parents, and pretending that they are acknowledged as such by their citizens. How authoritarian or liberal, Victorian or progressive, tough-minded or permissive they are is, in fact, not to the point at all. This dimension is in no way relevant to our problem, for the problem here is not just what sort of rules there should be, but how to get a proper contractual basis for whatever sort of rules there are.

A proper understanding of rules and contracts will issue in something that is of overwhelming importance for this whole area, something that education in this area is primarily out to generate: the *sincere acceptance* of certain contracts. This connects, both in theory and in practice, with other notions. If we sincerely accept a contract, and acknowledge the morally binding force of the rules it involves, it does not follow that we shall always keep the rules. But it does follow that we shall *repent* of our breach of the contract, *acknowledge* our error and be willing to make some kind of *restitution* for the damage done.

It is worth noting that these elements are commonly, and

43

horrifically, absent in many practical situations. This may be largely owing to the failure of educators and authorities to present pupils and citizens with a clearly defined and detailed contract, so that (one might say) they have no chance to make any such sincere acceptance – indeed, not much chance of grasping the concept of a contract at all. We are not anxious to apportion blame, and we shall pursue practical suggestions to remedy the situation later, but it exists. It is simply not the case that juvenile delinquents, rioters, law-breakers and pupils at school who contravene the rules have sincerely accepted the laws and rules that they transgress. The point emerges in the disparity between what a person may feel herself expected to say, and what she really thinks. One delinquent convicted of stealing said to the magistrate in court, 'Yeah, well, I'm sorry, I got carried away, I know it's wrong, I won't do it again.' Interviewed later, he said, 'I didn't make the ****ing rules. Some people have too much money anyway. I needed a new bike', and so forth.

A large number, not only of criminals, but of ordinary students and pupils are in what can only be described as a state of war in society. Not necessarily *against* society: not all of them feel that the 'they' who make the rules are trying to do down the 'we' who have to keep them, although such persecutory feelings are apt to be easily generated, and may be commonly found. But many people are, if not hostile to society, at least *disconnected* from it: the 'they' may not be regarded as tyrants, but are still dissociated from the 'we'. 'We' are the students, young people, the gang, the comparatively poor, the Catholics, the drop-outs. 'We' do not necessarily hate society, but 'we' are indifferent to it and do not regard ourselves as con-tractually bound by its laws. Some of 'us' may want to fight a 'hot war' with society, others a 'cold war'; others again merely profess total indifference.

We are accustomed to the difficulties of educating such people. We do not expect a high recovery rate from young offenders in institutions or prisons: the tender-minded of us regard them as mental cases whom it is not easy to cure, the tough-minded as hardened crooks or villains. But it is important to be clear what sort of situation we are dealing with, what sort of difficulties we have to overcome. It is *not*, in many cases, that such people lapse (however frequently) from a contract and set of rules that they acknowledge and accept. They do *not* think, in general and in their saner moments, that what they do is wrong. They may call it 'wrong' in inverted commas, meaning merely that it is liable to be punished, that 'society' or 'they' (the authorities) think it wrong, etc. But they do not think it wrong in the essential prescriptive sense of the word: that is, they have not *chosen* or *committed* themselves to trying to adjust their actual behaviour.

Because of this, the essential element in any kind of 'cure' or re-education is often missing. Quite simply, such people do not want to be 'cured' or re-educated: they prefer a situation in which they can carry on doing what they want, even if they sometimes get punished for it. They have formed their own norms and principles quite independently of any social contract or set of agreements. If the authorities are firm enough, they may be more effectively deterred from behaving in certain ways, but this does nothing to change their basic attitude. Moreover, as respect for the established authorities and for any moral consensus falls away, the strength of such deterrents has to increase in order to compensate for the loss of other motivation, and it is doubtful whether even such increased deterrents can be made strong, practical and effective enough to do the job. It is more sensible to tackle the problem in the educational field, and this means getting the sincere acceptance of contracts that we need.

CHAPTER 4
Authority and Education

So far we have tried to get a grip on the notion of authority in general, and the notion of discipline in general, without going too deeply into the particular relevance of these notions to *education*. We have seen that any social group, any group of human beings doing business together, requires the application of authority and discipline. But what sort of business is *educational* business? What is the place of authority in *education*?

To answer this, we have to look more closely at the enterprise of education. This is not an easy task, because there are disputes about the enterprise of education in a way that there are not disputes about (say) enterprises like car maintenance, curing leukaemia or sailing boats. In the latter, the nature and point of the enterprises are reasonably clear. There are obvious criteria of success – we know what counts as good car maintenance, or a proper cure for a disease, or sailing boats well. Consequently we recognize without too much difficulty who are the authorities or experts in these matters – expert mechanics, doctors or sailors. We also recognize the *scope* and *limits* of their authority; we would take the orders or advice of mechanics in matters affecting our cars, but not matters affecting our houses or pets; of doctors about our health, but not about our careers; of sailors about boats, but not about our private lives. But we are not so clear about the nature, point and limits of education and educational authority.

Some of the practical worries here emerge, again, in our pupils' minds. Here are some remarks and questions from pupils in the 11–16 age group:

> *You keep telling me what sort of clothes to wear, and not to use bad language: what's that got to do with learning anything? What's it to you if I say that seven sevens are ****ing 49?!?*

> *You say you're educating us, but as far as I can see you're taking over our lives altogether.*

*It's not education if you just **tell** us what to think, that's brain-washing.*

Who's to say what's good in education? It just depends what you think. Nazis thought they ought to learn how to put Jews in gas chambers.

What goes on in our school isn't education, it's just passing exams.

Oh yes, I had fun in Mr X's class, but I wasn't getting an education. You see, I wasn't really learning anything.

*When you say 'education' you just mean what goes in **your** school. I could be educated much better at home, or in the streets.*

Because of the deep controversies in and about education, quite a lot of teachers have despaired about trying to get clear about the enterprise, and unsurprisingly quite a lot of pupils have despaired as well. Pupils can too easily see it as just something that happens (or is supposed to happen) to them between nine in the morning and some time in the afternoon in a place called 'school'. There is not always, as there should be, the kind of agreement and harmony between teacher and pupil that come from a common understanding of a jointly undertaken enterprise – as there would be, for instance, between football players and a coach, or explorers and the leader of the expedition. And because of this, the authority of the teacher or educator is not commonly agreed either. It is as if different people were playing quite different games on the same board. That sort of confusion engenders despair, which in turn engenders chaos and conflict. So, again, we need clarity and understanding.

Ought we to start, then, by 'defining' education? Something turns here on what is to count as 'defining'. Many people nowadays are reluctant, perhaps with some justice, to talk about the 'definition', the 'essence', of education, and it is true that a very great deal has been written under headings like 'the aims of education', 'the nature of education', 'the concept of education' and so on, most of which is more confusing than helpful. It is better to start by asking ourselves what it is that such discussions are attempting to clarify, why we *need* to consider the 'concept' or the 'nature' of education. Suppose we are teachers, educational administrators, researchers or civil servants in some ministry of education: what is the point of engaging in reflection about education?

To this question the answer is reasonably clear, we think. It is, quite simply, so that we can have an adequate and consciously held view about what we are trying to do, about the nature of the enterprise in which we are engaging. Now, of course, actual people in actual jobs – teachers, civil servants and so on – will be engaged from time to time in many different enterprises. A teacher does not only teach: he or she may also keep the register, referee sports matches, attend union meetings and so on, and in time of war or some other crisis he or she may have to keep the pupils safe from bombs or plague. Similarly, a doctor does not only cure people: she may also have to fill in forms, keep accounts, tidy her consulting room and all sorts of other things. But we (rightly) have the feeling that there is some enterprise with which these people are, or ought to be, specially connected, something that is central to what they do. Just as doctors are concerned primarily with medicine and promoting health, so (we may feel) teachers and others are, or ought to be, primarily engaged in the enterprise of educating.

This feeling, so far vaguely expressed, does not allow us to conclude that the other enterprises are unimportant or ought somehow to be got rid of. Plainly, much will depend on circumstance. If we are attacked by barbarians or do not have enough to eat, it will no doubt be sensible for teachers (and perhaps even doctors) to stop teaching (curing) and turn their attention to finding food for themselves and other people or to fending off enemy attacks. The feeling is rather that there are *in principle* – 'in theory' if you like, though we hope also in practice – enterprises with a nature that just *is* different. Educating people is one thing, curing them is another, keeping them properly fed is yet another, and so on. We have different words that fairly mark these enterprises (education, medicine, agriculture), but the words in themselves may not give us a sufficient grasp of what the enterprises are and how they differ from each other. For the enterprises exist in their own right (in principle or in theory), whether or not people identify them clearly with certain words. Even if people did not identify them or practise them at all, they would still be important: the enterprises we call science, medicine and democracy are important in themselves, even though many societies may have had no understanding of them and lived by superstition, witch-doctoring and tyranny.

There are two general temptations that need special notice. The first lies in identifying an enterprise that exists in its own right with particular social practices or institutions. To take a parallel: human beings may engage in an activity or enterprise that we may want to call 'religion' (although, no doubt, we are not entirely clear just what this enterprise is). It would be wrong to think that this is the same as saying that certain people and social practices – parsons, funerals, churches and so on – actually exist or even that there are certain sets of beliefs and doctrines that are called 'religious'. For we could always ask, 'Are these people (institutions, beliefs, etc.), whatever they may be *called*, actually concerned with religion?', and we may often find that they are not. If we identify religion with certain social practices, we make the same mistake as the man who is humorously quoted as saying, 'When I say religion of course I mean the Christian religion, and when I say the Christian religion of course I mean the Church of England'. The point is not just that the man is prejudiced: it is that he has no idea of religion as an enterprise in its own right.

It is the same with the notion of educating people. We may call certain things schools and certain people teachers. We may say that what we are doing is to educate children; but we have to be able to show that this is, in fact, what we are doing. The mere existence of social practices with the word education attached to them indicates nothing, any more than, in the police state of Orwell's *Nineteen Eighty-Four*, the naming of an institution as the ministry of Truth proved that the institution was, in fact, concerned with truth (rather than, as Orwell represents it, with propaganda). It is a very open question as to how much education goes on in those institutions that we currently classify under that heading. Clearly, we cannot answer the question until we know, or decide, what 'education' is to signify; but equally we cannot assume that the answer is provided by existing institutions.

The second temptation is to use (or abuse) 'education' to endorse not a particular set of social practices but some particular ideal or set of values that we happen to favour. Most writers on the subject have some general ideology, 'doctrine of man', or political or moral theory that they want to sell, and their 'educational theory' (together with what they want 'education' to mean) exists chiefly as a kind of spin-off, so to speak, from this general idea. The same temptations beset words (in any language) that signify enterprises of a fairly general nature, which we have not taken the trouble to get clear: religion, politics, morals and many others. They lure us to endorse either existing social practices or our own partisan views (and these two may obviously be connected with each other more closely than we have here made apparent).

As far as we can see, these and other similar manoeuvres are not only mistaken but also largely unnecessary. There is a concept that, when properly explained, makes tolerably clear the kind of enterprise we need to distinguish and (although this is, in one way, a secondary consideration) best fits the term 'educate' as it is now normally used by English speakers (and other parallel terms that exist in other languages). To state this as briefly as possible: 'education' is the marker for a particular enterprise or activity, which has as its aim or 'good' the sustained and serious learning of rational creatures, planned in some coherent or overall way. We educate people (rather than treating them in other ways) when we are engaged in bringing such learning about; and people become educated when, or in so far as, they have done some learning of the kind.

Compared with the particular pictures presented by most authors, this is a fairly broad concept, but it is, we think, the concept that most contemporary English speakers denote by the term 'education'. There is some limitation on the learning that will count as education. We do not use the term of trivial or fragmentary bits of learning, nor of the learning of animals or infants, but we do use it where what is learned may be undesirable (bad habits, hatred of Jews or plenty of other things) and where the amount of knowledge or understanding is very small (one can learn, in a serious and sustained way, to acquire certain habits, skills or attitudes without much knowledge attached to them). We speak of *bad* (that is, not incompetent but evil) education, just as we can speak of bad religion, bad moral principles, bad political ideals and so on. We have to distinguish these from cases that are not cases of religion, morality or politics at all – and also from cases of education that does not involve much knowledge or understanding.

This (very brief) sketch needs to be supplemented by two elaborations. First, some limitation, not so much of content as of general intention, is placed on the concept of education by virtue of the fact that education is a general or comprehensive kind of enterprise. Thus the *Oxford English Dictionary* speaks of education as 'systematic instruction, schooling or training', and for educate gives 'to bring up (young persons) from childhood so as to form (their) habits, manners, intellectual and physical aptitudes'. Not just any learning counts as education: the learning has to be seen as part of a systematic and coherent enterprise. Hence the grammar of 'to educate' is different from the grammar of (for instance) 'to train'. We can train people in particular skills, for particular tasks or as fillers of particular roles, but we can only educate *people as such*. If we claim to educate people, we claim to be viewing their learning from some general, overall or comprehensive point of view, not *just* with an eye to certain jobs or skills.

Of course, since people have minds, and since education consists of learning, it is likely that a large part of this enterprise will be seen as the development of knowledge and understanding in people; indeed, an educational ideal that involved no such development would be hard to conceive. Yet one might easily think that the really important things for people to learn – still in a comprehensive and coherent sort of way – did not involve much intellectual or cognitive sophistication but were more in the area marked by character, habits, attitudes and so on. One might believe that these things were best learned by imitation, practice, exhortation, games-playing or other methods of that kind. Again, one might think it rash to lay down any particular content as being 'really important' for *all* pupils – such content might reasonably vary according to each pupil's particular needs and abilities. But the notion of education is neutral with regard to any questions of content: as long as there is an enterprise of this general kind, the term 'education' cannot be rejected.

Secondly, 'education' is normally a fairly formal, structured or institutionalized enterprise, something designed to raise people above the level of what they would naturally learn for themselves in the ordinary course of events. We do not speak of parents and other language users educating their children, or even teaching them to talk, if the children just pick up the use of language from the adults – even though this learning may be thought crucially important for any mental development. We may, indeed, loosely say that certain people or experiences exercise an 'educational' effect, but 'educate' is a much narrower term than 'bring up', 'rear' or 'nurture'.

These are at least some of the issues that would emerge from a thorough and systematic study of how words are actually used.

Much more work, in our judgement, needs to be done in this field, both on English words and on those terms that are, at least prima facie, parallel in other natural languages. But whatever may or may not be true of English and other usage, the important point is that a particular kind of enterprise exists that needs to be delimited in this way because it is concerned with a certain kind of 'good' – namely, learning. There are, of course, still wider concepts: 'upbringing', say, or 'what we do for children' would include a number of very different goods. At one time we are concerned with our children's health, at another with their appearance and so on. Learning, though a broad enough idea, represents only one kind of interest and this interest is not confined to children. A variety of other terms normally goes along with this particular interest; we would not refer to children as pupils, for instance, nor to adults as teachers, unless we had this interest in mind.

There are other enterprises concerned with other specific goods, as we have already noted, and it is important to see that each of these is delimited or bounded in the same sort of way. Often this is clear to us: we know pretty well when we do something to a person for medical reasons, and we can distinguish these from educational or (say) economic reasons. A sick man may have to retire from attending university or from his business: this may be good for his health but bad for his education or his pocket. Sometimes, partly because of a lack of clarity about the terms and concepts in question, we are less clear. But whatever we choose to label as politics, morals or (to take a currently fashionable term) ideology, we must, if these terms are to have any clear meaning, be able to distinguish a political (moral, ideological) reason for doing something from another kind of reason, which means that we must be able to distinguish it from an educational reason.

In fact, if we resist the temptation to extend terms like political (moral, ideological, etc.) to cover more or less any consideration, we can already do this in many cases. It is politically desirable that when attacked by barbarians we should not worry too much about learning things but should devote our attention to keeping our society safe. It is morally desirable that if Romans are in danger of being burned alive, we should at least put off learning the violin until we have done what we can to help them. It is, or may be, 'ideologically' desirable (although we are not entirely clear what 'ideologically' means) that children from different social backgrounds should belong to the same school or the same housing estate; but whether this improves these children's learning may be another matter.

It is for these reasons that the concept of education, as we have tried to delimit it, cannot sensibly be seen as contestable, dependent on one's ultimate values or anything of that kind, any more than can the concept of medicine, with its connected good (health). Indeed, we can go somewhat further than this. The enterprise of education is plainly necessary for any human society or individual, a point largely masked by those authors who prefer to adopt a much more stringent and value-impregnated concept and have to try to justify it. The reason is that we could not come to resemble anything much like rational creatures unless we had done a good deal of serious and sustained learning, and it is implausible to suppose that such learning could be successfully done if it were left entirely to chance and nature. Some general or overall attempt, on a more or less broad front, to advance children's learning – whatever we may think it important to learn – seems essential, if only because natural ability and circumstance are unreliable. In much the same way, an enterprise devoted to keeping people fit and healthy (that is, medicine) will be an inevitable feature of almost any society, even if different societies vary in their ideas of what counts as fitness or health, as they certainly vary in their ideas of how to achieve it.

Whether or not this sort of delimitation is acceptable as a definition of education does not ultimately matter all that much as long as we are clear about, and agree on, what verbal markers we are attaching to which enterprises. Few people will deny the importance of sustained and serious learning, even though they might dispute the delimitation, and even though they might disagree about what ought to be learned. But we are not always as clear as we should be about the logical or conceptual requirements that the notion of sustained and serious learning itself imposes on us and that we have to attend to if our educational practice is to prosper. There is real danger that, under pressure from other (non-educational) sources, teachers and educators may lose their grip on what must be regarded as central at least to the notion of education.

There are two general ways in which an enterprise can be corrupted: by external pressure and by internal irrationality.

It may be that because of external pressures or desires that conflict with the enterprise, 'society' – or some group of power holders – does not give the necessary powers to those who should be conducting it. In so far as the Soviet Communist Party told biologists what they were to think, or painters how they were to paint, to that extent biology and painting became corrupted. If administrators and porters do not allow doctors the scope and power necessary to conduct operations and otherwise treat their patients as the doctors think best, to that extent medicine is impossible. Similarly, if there is no class of people who are empowered to educate – who are charged with the making of educational decisions and trusted to use the time and money involved as they think best without fear of outside pressure – education becomes difficult or impossible. If a Gestapo agent, a Party commissar, a 'democratic consensus', an educational fashion, or parental or bureaucratic pressure is breathing down the educator's neck, and telling him or her what to do, he or she cannot do the job satisfactorily. The position becomes impossible for the enterprise, just as chess-playing cannot flourish if politicians tell chess-players what moves to make.

The people most plausibly to be identified as educators, and therefore to be given the relevant powers, are the *teachers* because, briefly, they have a better grasp of the knowledge and other things to be learned and they are personally familiar with the students who are doing the learning. We do not, of course, deny that both parents and society have some rights here – for instance, to insist that students at least learn to be economically and socially viable – but within certain fairly obvious limits the enterprise must be conducted by those on the spot and in the know. The educators must have whatever disciplinary powers they need: sufficient powers to order the curriculum, the organization of the school and the methods of teaching; powers over the spending of whatever money society can afford to devote to education; powers to ensure the sanctity and potency of the school (college, university), if necessary in the teeth of social or political pressures; and powers to ensure the educability of their pupils (which include at least certain powers over the home environment). All these seem notoriously lacking in our society – and, indeed, in any society we know.

Even if these powers are granted, it is always possible, of course, that the educators themselves may lose a proper grip on their own enterprise. The may become affected by various types of irrationality. Some educational theory or educational research shows this irrationality. It arises chiefly from various beliefs about the human mind, which issue in forms that are, or should be, well-known: a belief in behaviourism and behavioural objectives, the regarding of almost any attribute as a 'skill', an addiction to a particular sociology or ideology, or the characteristically liberal guilt that makes us dismiss or play down ideas denoted by punishment, examination or competition.

Human beings are, we think, susceptible to irrationality in any social system; indeed, social systems usually do little more than echo and institutionalize the types of irrationality to which all individuals are liable. It is important to ensure that the external pressures are checked in order that education may have at least the chance of flourishing, but it is equally important that the tendencies to internal corruption are also checked in order that it may actually flourish. For that reason we believe that, however much light may be shed on the external, sociological or institutional forces that make education difficult, these forces will continue to flourish in one form or another as long as the basic fantasies continue to dominate us. It thus seems to be ultimately itself an educational issue; enough influential individuals need to understand the nature of the enterprise and its necessary conditions, and to gain sufficient control over their fantasies, to ensure that their intellects do not renege on what they have learned philosophically. This applies particularly to teachers themselves.

It is not surprising that education is today a natural stamping ground both for political and bureaucratic pressure and for inner irrationality. There are obvious reasons why education attracts both the earnest technologically minded bureaucrat and the idealist acting out his or her own compulsions. The really tiresome thing about this is that it masks the extent to which education, if allowed and encouraged to flourish, could change things for the better: an intuition that the 'great educators' of the past at least kept alive. If we could really teach people not only to be socially viable but also to become seriously attached to what is worth while, to conduct their moral lives with at worst competence and at best imagination and enthusiasm, to be able genuinely to love at least some other people

55

(if only their own children), to find some genuine joy, excitement and contentment in life – if we could do any or all of these things, we would at least have some idea of the enormous power that education has in principle. That it does not wield this power in practice is not, we are sure, primarily because of intellectual incompetence, lack of research or lack of economic or technological resources; it is because we do not give the enterprise a fair chance.

Hence it is difficult, in this age, to say very much about the positive possibilities of education. They sound futuristic or Utopian. In much the same way, it would have been difficult in the Middle Ages to talk of the 'wonders of science' or to make clear what benefits the properly constituted and fantasy-free practice of medicine would bring, because at that time these two enterprises were hemmed about with enemies that made their proper practice impossible. So it is with education now: it is apparent, here and there (in those rare cases where educators are both properly empowered and themselves uncorrupted), just how enormous are the benefits it can bring. In a (real if imprecise) sense, anyone who has ever had a loving parent or teacher knows well enough what education can do. But such cases are not common enough. We do not see many teachers with the influence of Socrates or Dr Arnold. (Who would hire Socrates nowadays? And would Thomas Arnold have tolerated the administrators and bureaucrats of today?) We have, as it were, a vague if precious glimpse of what education might be, if given a fair chance. That glimpse is worth hanging on to, although perhaps not much is gained by singing hymns to it. What we have to do, first and foremost, is to clear the ground – to make the enterprise possible. Then we will have some chance of studying it, and conducting it sensibly.

CHAPTER 5
Authority and Morality

The notion of authority has important connections with morality, and we want here to look at some of the mistakes commonly made. The mistakes masquerade as theories or ideas about how morality should be practised. They are really escapes from the real world, escapes from *thinking* about authority and morality. We list here eight different things that people commonly find themselves doing instead of thinking.

OBEYING AND REBELLING

Obeying One easy escape from thinking is to stop thinking and do something else – namely, *obey* uncritically. Such obeying is, for many people, psychologically easier than thinking, just as it is rather relaxing, in a way, to be in the army where you are told what to do and just go ahead and do it, instead of having to make up your own mind. Some people find relief from thinking in obeying a boss, or their husbands or wives, or the commands of some leader-figure (Churchill, Hitler or Mao Tse-tung) or the biggest child in the gang: others have some kind of God whom they obey and whose will they try to do. All this is rather like children obeying their parents. Often they may obey a book of rules (the Bible, the sayings of Mao) laid down by the authority, which comes to much the same thing.

Rebelling This is like obeying, but the opposite. Some people, instead of deliberately acting in a certain way because some authority wants them to, deliberately act in the opposite way just because some authority does not want them to. Such people are just as much obsessed with authority as those who obey, like children who disobey their parents simply in order to show their independence. Young people who need to prove to themselves that they are independent often behave like this. They break rules and conventions, not because they really think in each particular case that this is the reasonable thing to do, but to show to themselves and to the outside world that they are not going to do things just because someone tells them to.

'IDEAL PEOPLE'

Another easy escape is to get hold of some ideal person – someone you admire – and try to imitate him or her. (This, too, is rather like what children do with their parents.) Some people admire saint-like people – St Francis, Mother Teresa, Gandhi. Others have stronger heroes like Churchill or Lenin. Others again admire more obvious heroic achievements, like those of Edmund Hilary or Scott or Francis Chichester. Others admire heroic reformers, like Dr Arnold or Florence Nightingale. Yet others admire film or TV stars, pop singers, football players, or just people who are strong or good-looking or rich and successful. Here too, there is nothing wrong with admiring the right people, but you have to be sure that they *are* the right people, and this means thinking.

'PURPOSE' AND 'MEANING'

Quite a lot of people have some belief, not so much in a personal God to obey or imitate, but in some spirit of the universe, life-force, divine law or whatever. They talk as if the universe was almost a person: 'the *purpose* of the universe is . . .', 'human beings were *meant* to be . . .', and so on. This is like a watered-down religion, and is used like a religion to avoid thinking about what one really ought to be or do. Having this picture helps people to feel that the 'answer' to life is something *given* or *laid down*, not something that people can choose, sensibly or unreasonably, for themselves.

'SPECIAL EXPERIENCES'

Many people put their money on some kind of 'special' experience which they take as having some sort of importance or authority. A good example, but one which is not regarded as very respectable nowadays, is seeing a vision. Hearing a voice, as Joan of Arc is supposed to have done, is another. Nowadays people talk more of 'what my conscience tells me', 'my intuition', or say 'I just some-how feel that . . .'. Or they say things like 'when a man is near death, then he *knows*', or 'when you're alone with Nature, some-how you can *see* that . . .'. Of course experiences of all kinds are useful and important but we have to think in order to evaluate them. (To put it in religious language, a voice may be from God or the devil.)

'FAITH'

Another reaction – another way of defending ourselves against thinking – is to say things like 'reason can only get you so far; after that you have to make the leap of faith', or 'you have to rely on intuition'. This is really only a rather stronger version of the last defence we looked at. It says, in effect, that because you believe something, what you believe must be right or true. A lot of words, like faith, revelation or intuition, are used to cover up this idea, which in its naked form is obviously silly; and there are a great many occasions when people say things like 'Well, you may argue as much as you like, but I just *know* that . . .'. What is missing here is the notion of *giving reasons* for beliefs. If we abandon this notion, there is really nothing to distinguish sane human beings from lunatics. A lunatic believes something but has no good reason for believing it. To be willing to give reasons, to have your beliefs out in public, to allow them to be inspected and challenged, is essential for all kinds of thinking.

'A MATTER OF TASTE'

Then there are those whose way of giving up thinking is becoming increasingly respectable nowadays. They talk as if there are no reasonable principles or standards at all: 'it's all a matter of taste'. They believe, in effect, what suits them (or what they think suits them), and have no desire to think about whether what they believe is *right* or *true*. These people are governed not by any authority, ideal, etc., but simply by their own mental state, by what they find easiest to believe, or by their own particular desires and feelings. Such people really mean, 'The whole thing is so difficult, I just can't face finding out what's right, so let's drop the subject.'

'HOW YOU HAVE BEEN BROUGHT UP'

Yet another defence is to say something like, 'Well, it all depends what you've been brought up to believe, doesn't it?' The idea is that if, for instance, you've been brought up to believe that there is a God, or that sleeping with people before you're married is wrong, that settles it – there isn't any need to think about it. But although how you've been brought up obviously does make a great difference to what you believe, it does not give you good *reasons* for believing it. If a Nazi who had been brought up to kill Jews said, 'Well, I was brought up that way, there's no point in our arguing about it', we should not accept this as a defence. Indeed, we should think him doubly wrong: first, he is wrong about how to treat Jews, and secondly, he is not open to argument. He has resigned from being a reasonable human being; he is no longer open to criticism, or able to change his mind. He is not very far from being mad.

OTHER PEOPLE

A great many people take the 'answers to life' for granted by doing and thinking what their friends do and think. Nearly everyone has some group of people whom he or she accepts and by whom he or she is accepted (what sociologists call a 'peer group'), usually people of the same social class, with similar outlooks and pursuits. It is assumed that what these people think, and how they act, is right; or if not right, at least not seriously wrong. Phrases like 'decent people', 'right-thinking people', 'properly brought-up people' and so on are used here. The thoughts and actions of the peer group vary from group to group: they may include fox-hunting or listening to pop music, liking or disliking people with a different skin colour, having long or short hair, using this or that accent and vocabulary, and having this or that set of manners and conventions. Note that the peer group may not only actually *set* the standards i.e. give its individual members ready-made 'answers' to what is right and wrong, but also *reinforce* and *support* the individual's standards. If almost everyone in the group admires the same 'great woman' or obeys the same authorities, then not much serious thinking and discussion is likely to get done.

All these people have put the 'goodness' (which we all seek) *outside* their own intelligence, reason or conscious control. Some install it in an authority (a leader, their friends, fashion), some in their own desires, impulses and feelings. The process can be regarded essentially as an escape from reason, in one form or another, and it is remarkable (if predictable) that in the area of morality and religion many people can still be found to dismiss or degrade human rationality. 'Why should I be reasonable?', 'reason only carries you so far', 'you need faith', 'ultimately it's a matter of how you feel'. All these bear witness to this desire to escape from what in our saner moods we all know perfectly well to be our task – namely, to understand and control our lives in the moral area as in other areas.

For 'reason' or 'being reasonable' is only another way of talking about *facing the real world*, and using evidence rather than our own fantasies to deal with it. If a person were to deny this in areas like science, history or mathematics, we should (rightly) think him or her misguided, or in the extreme case a bit mad. 'I don't care about evidence or reasoning, I just somehow feel that the sun goes round the earth', or 'my intuition just tells me that William the Conqueror landed in 1066', sound very odd to us. But in morality and religion people get away with saying such things: it is still respectable to talk of faith, intuition, etc. as if these were alternative ways of understanding.

Ultimately the only alternative for us is to have some kind of commitment to the processes of reasoning, discussion, considering evidence and so on. We have to see these as interesting, important, 'good', worthwhile and valuable. We have to invest some emotion, not in our particular fantasies or moral views, but in the business of examining and evaluating them – in the business of *thinking*. Of course this requires a degree of maturity that not everyone enjoys all the time, but nearly everyone is capable of some investment of this kind, which can be increased with practice and effort. It is a great gain to appreciate what our policy ought to be, even if we often lack the strength to pursue it, and we can form the habit, or initiate ourselves into the tradition, of at least attempting to approach things reasonably rather than merely letting off emotional steam.

Can we go a bit further in considering how to tackle our temptations about morality and authority? Perhaps we can, if we are clear about the *directions* in which we can go. One direction is to make clear the *proper* basis of authority for morals. That is important, just as it is important to recognize the proper and truly authoritative procedures for dealing with other areas of life (science, history, etc.). But that direction has limitations, since many people will not even listen to, much less try to run their lives by, these principles. There are far more temptations against doing morality properly than against doing science properly. Some educators, again, take particular moral problems, perhaps rather difficult ones – about politics, sex, war or censorship, for instance – and try to apply the principles we have learned. Now although this is interesting and can be useful, it is likely to be largely a waste of time. For it is pretty plain that people's opinions about such problems are mostly a product of their own prejudices: the opinions just reflect their own emotions, their social background, the way they were brought up, and so on. It is the *emotions* and *attitudes* that are all-important here. Unless we can get at these, a lot of argument and discussion is superficial and unhelpful.

We recognize this well enough in some cases. For instance, it often seems to us as if *arguments* about religion, politics or sex are pointless, because the people arguing have too much emotion invested in their point of view: they are not really open to conviction, not really anxious to discover what is true or what is morally right. They want to let off steam, or prove to themselves (as well as to others) that what they *feel* is somehow respectable. Often they do not really *think* at all, and often what look like moral or religious beliefs and opinions aren't really beliefs and opinions – they are just expressions of the person's own feeling. The amount of serious moral thinking that goes on is actually very small indeed.

This does not apply only to the obvious cases, as when a person just shouts, 'You ****ing Jew!' or '**** you, you ****ing communist!', or calls policemen 'pigs', or has a row with his or her parents, or anything of that kind. It applies also to cases where a person may seem very calm and cool, but in fact he has his own feelings and is not going to change them – nor is he going to change the 'opinions' based on them. A person may bluster and shout and say, 'My God, young people today are going to the dogs: look at their foul clothes and horrible long hair, and the way they behave sexually, just like animals – they need their bottoms smacked, what we want is more discipline.' But he may also be very calm and say something like, 'Yes, well, of course we all know that sex is wrong outside marriage, that hair should be cut short and people should wear 'proper' clothes. . . . ' In both cases the speaker gives himself away because he has made up his mind already: he has his feelings and pretends (to himself) that he *knows* something. He is not being *serious* about morality, because he is really only interested in his own feelings.

In just the same way a young person may shout and swear at

adults: 'The stupid ****ing fools, they don't understand, what right have they . . .?', or just flare up in anger when she talks to a parent, teacher or someone in authority. But she may also say, 'Yes, well, the poor old adults are completely past it, the world has changed too much, there's absolutely no point in listening to anything *they* have to say.' This is really just as bad, because it is just as unreasonable and just as much a mere reflection of the speaker's feelings. Anyone who sat down and *seriously* asked the question, 'Is what adults have to say worth listening to?' would be more or less bound to answer, 'Yes, at least sometimes'. No other answer is possible – *if* you ask the question seriously. But if you're just anxious to repeat your own feelings to yourself, then of course you won't be asking questions and seeking for answers at all. You will just be having a game with yourself; really, just trying to reassure yourself.

This is why morality is difficult. It is not that we have mistaken views or think inaccurately about these problems. It is rather that we too often do not really have *views* or *think* or treat them as *problems* at all. In a sense, we cannot afford to: our emotions are so strong, and we feel so insecure, that we have to follow our own feelings – it is a kind of compulsion, rather like being hypnotized, indoctrinated or brainwashed.

To pick up what we have just said, it sometimes seems as if people are serious about morals, politics, religion and such things just because they get very emotional about it: they speak forcefully, often angrily; they talk as if it mattered very much; they are earnest, feel strongly, and so on. Of course there is a sense in which they are serious: that is, they are not just joking. But it is important to realize that they are not often serious *about anything in the real world*. What they are serious about is their own feelings.

This is very common in other cases. A boy may say, 'Oh, I absolutely worship Jane. Of course I'm serious, I love her very much.' Now of course his feelings are serious; but often we wonder, 'Does he actually love *Jane*? Is it *that girl*, with her particular character and ideas, her thoughts and feelings, that he's interested in and claims to love? Does he really love *her* – isn't it rather that he loves some picture or image of her that he has in himself? If he doesn't really know and understand her properly, how can he love her?' Or in an even simpler case, someone may say, 'Oh, I love children and animals', but often it turns out that what is loved is just the *idea* of children and animals – the person is not really *interested* in them, does not want to look after them, does not really know anything about them.

To be serious about something involves more than just being enthusiastic about the idea of it. Above all, it involves having *respect* for it. If we are serious about (say) cooking, then we do not just go ahead and cook: we *learn* about it, try out various dishes and collect opinions about them, sample other people's cooking for comparison, find things out from the really good or 'professional' cooks, and so on. It is not a matter of having *feelings* about being a cook or cooking; it is a matter of having respect for the activity *in itself*. To be serious about politics is not just a matter of having strong views and acting on them. It involves learning and thinking about politics, trying to reach correct conclusions, considering various points of view and so on.

Being serious about anything is difficult, and being serious about morality is very difficult: indeed that *is* the difficulty about morality. It is difficult because having respect for something – a person, an activity, a subject of study, or anything else – means being able to give up one's own personal feelings in favour of the thing itself. You have to let go of your own feelings about the thing, and (as it were) let the thing speak to you itself in its own way. For example, if you are trying to look at a piece of music seriously, you have to overcome your initial responses and reactions: you have to get beyond just saying 'I like that', 'this is boring', 'that's marvellous', etc., and try to understand it for what it is, or what the composer meant it to be. You have to 'get inside' the music, which involves forgetting yourself. If you are serious about a person, you have to let that person exist in his or her own right: it is fatal if you load your own feelings on to him or her, because then you do not give yourself the chance to understand what *that person* is actually like.

This is where the trouble comes in morality. For only too often we cannot, or will not, forget ourselves enough, so that we do not give ourselves the chance even to *look straight at* other people and moral situations. There is a sense in which being 'selfish' or 'self-centred' is the only real enemy. But this does not only (or even chiefly) mean that we want more than our fair share, or that we are not self-sacrificing or 'good' enough. It means that we are too bound up with ourselves, too anxious about our own feelings and our own situation, to have enough time and energy to spare for considering anything in the outside world. (Some unlucky children are so tied up with themselves that they hardly realize that the outside world is there at all. They are given a special name, autistic children, but really this is something that all of us suffer from to some extent.) We are in effect deaf and blind to anything except what is going on in ourselves, and even that we do not look at seriously.

It is important to realize that this is, in one sense anyway, *our own fault*. We have here to beware of two mistakes, both very common and both ways of trying to escape from the truth. If someone is bad-tempered, careless or prejudiced, or has some other fault (as we all have) which prevents her from being serious about moral situations, and this is pointed out to her, she may easily take one of two lines.

She may say, 'Yes, it's true, but I can't help it, it's not my fault. I just *am* a bad-tempered (careless, etc.) person, there's nothing I can do about it. All my family are like it, I expect it's in the blood, or it's to do with how I've been brought up,' and so on. This is a cheat, because she is not really seeing her bad temper as part of *her*, something that *she* is and is responsible for. She seems to think of her bad temper as if it were like the colour of her skin or her hair, something she has been landed with and cannot do anything about.

She may say, 'Yes, it's very wrong of me. I do indeed feel guilty about it and ought to be punished. I know I've been naughty (bad),' and so on. This is often a cheat too, because she is not really trying to look at or *understand* her bad temper or carelessness. She just owns up to it, gets punished or blamed, and then carries on as before. She sees it as 'being naughty', not as something that is *wrong with her*, some part of her character or mind that needs looking at seriously and altering. Again it is not really *her*, just the 'naughty' part of her.

Both these are ways of escape, ways of shrugging off the fact that *we* are wrong, or muddled inside ourselves, or (in a way) ill. Religious people sometimes use the word 'sin' to describe this situation, and whatever we think of religion, it is a situation we have to acknowledge if we are to make any progress. It is not a matter of being naughty or disobedient, or breaking the rules, or being immoral, and it is not a matter either of having had bad luck, as someone might have a crippled arm or a bald head. It is *part of us*, a central feature of what *we are*; and we have to take responsibility for it.

Let us look now at some of the typical ways we feel and behave, when we are not always being reasonable or serious about morality. Before we list them we need to say: that these patterns *are not good or bad in themselves*, they are just patterns of human emotions that, being human, we all have; that this will not be, in any sense, a complete or well-ordered list – that would be an enormous and difficult task, so we will leave it to teachers to add other items to the list. Given that, most of the following items can be recognized fairly easily by most people.

There are a lot of things we can say about these patterns. They overlap with each other, and often the same emotion appears in many patterns. But it will be best just to list them, at this stage, and say things about them afterwards. We will give examples that fall into three rough groups.

AGGRESSION

These are patterns that we use when our instinctive response is to *fight* or *tackle* the situation, rather than withdrawing from it or trying to escape. It is one way of trying to cope with difficulties in life.

Lashing out at life   At times people lash out, with violence or at least with force. Sometimes they seem to do it aimlessly, as when vandals and hooligans go around smashing windows, beating people up or generally throwing their weight about. Sometimes the same force or violence comes out in a more sensible form, as when someone plays football hard or does something worth doing with determination or enthusiasm. The violence then becomes a virtue. All of us feel annoyed or angry or even furious at times. But we are not always angry about something in particular. Underlying this anger, sometimes, is a general feeling of rage and frustration at life. We feel impotent, powerless, unable to make a dent in the world. So we lash out.

Attacking authority   There are times – many times – when we resent authority: the authority of parents, teachers, policemen and so on. So we lash out at authorities in particular. Sometimes this is sensible: sometimes the authority needs to be attacked, because it is unjust. A lot of very virtuous people have used up a great deal of energy in defying the authorities, in a just cause. They stand up for free speech, for oppressed peoples or for some other worthwhile thing (not for themselves). Sometimes it is not sensible, and we lash out at authorities just because they are authorities and we do not like them. Again, there is likely to be an underlying feeling of inferiority and impotence behind this, or perhaps a feeling of envy. It is very hard to tell when a person is attacking authority justly or unjustly. Consider examples of attitudes to teachers, parents, the police and so on.

Trying to prove oneself   If you feel impotent, small, insecure (as we all do at times), you may 'try to prove yourself'. You try to make yourself seem 'ideal', or behave as if you were in fact big or powerful or successful. It is reassuring if you can pretend to yourself in this way. A boy might pretend that he is an 'ideal man', a girl that she is an 'ideal woman'. Again, you can do this sensibly or stupidly. It all depends on whether the ideal is a good one, and on whether you take sensible steps to be like the ideal. Some people reassure themselves in silly ways – for instance, bullying people smaller than themselves, joining a gang and beating up other people, or dressing up in clothes that they do no really like but feel they must wear because they are fashionable. Others are more reasonable and try to achieve real things – they try to learn more, to become more skilled at something or to help other people more.

Trying to get attention   If you feel small and unwanted, there are other ways you can adopt than violence or trying to prove yourself. You can try to get attention. For instance, you can do something different just for the sake of doing something different, you can make an unnecessary fuss about something, you can always be late for things or you can be the 'funny one' of the group, the professional clown, never taking things seriously. These are not very good ways of getting attention. There are better ways. You can ask for help when you need it and give it to other people when they need it, or you can try to do or be something other people like. This may seem harder work.

Wanting to lead   Wanting to lead other people, or tell others what to do, is common to all of us. Some find themselves taking this role easily: they have no hesitation in saying 'come on, we'll do this', 'we'll go there' or 'hey, do so-and-so'. This desire to dominate and control is acceptable in some circumstances (if you are captain of a ship, for instance) but not in others (if you are just a member of the crew). Often it is better to say 'what about doing this?', 'how do you feel about going there?' or 'wouldn't it be a good idea to do so-and-so?'. You can lead without bullying. Having the feeling that so-and-so ought to be done is quite all right: it is what you do with the emotion that makes your behaviour just or unjust, selfish or kind.

Being 'naughty'   Everyone has been brought up to 'be good', in the way our parents and others see 'being good'. At times we resent this and want to do the opposite. For instance, if we have been brought up not to use swear words, not to masturbate or have sex with people, to be clean and neatly dressed, and so on, we may come to rebel against this from time to time. So we get a kick out of being naughty: using 'bad' language, having scruffy clothes, and so on. There may well be nothing wrong with the behaviour involved in being naughty, just as there may not be anything really right with being good. It all depends on whether we are in *control* of this (natural) desire to escape from the way we have been brought up. If we *use* the desire to work out our own views of right and wrong, that is excellent; if we are just blindly *impelled* by the desire to do the opposite of what our parents, etc. said, that is boring.

Ganging up against something   If there is something or someone we dislike, or fear, or want to attack, we often gang up against it: that is, we join a group of other people for the purpose of attacking it. Our ancestors would gang up to fight their enemies, or to kill a lion. Birds and other animals gang up against other groups – human beings often do the same. There is safety in numbers, and they feel more powerful and able to express their aggression in a gang. Lots of groups are like this: not only real gangs or groups (gangs of skinheads, the Mafia, etc.), but also religious and political groups. Girls sometimes get together and form groups *against* other girls, or against the authorities. Equally there are more useful groups, like hockey teams, gangs of workmen doing a job or a team of social workers. These are *against* something, but not against other people. They try to tackle a problem, play an enjoyable game or help each other. It all depends on how you use the feeling of security that comes from ganging up.

WITHDRAWING

These patterns represent another general way of coping with life – not by fighting, but by withdrawing. In these moods we feel that the best thing to do (or the only thing to do) is to give up, accept things as they are or somehow keep out of the way.

Placating authority   Instead of lashing out at authority we can placate it: that is, we can try to keep the authorities happy by doing what they want. Of course this is often, perhaps usually, sensible. But much depends on the spirit in which we do it, and what it is that we are placating them about. Placating really means 'trying to keep someone from being angry'. If we do this *just* because we are scared, we may sometimes go wrong; or perhaps we want to do something good that will make the authorities angry, and it is best if we do it and let them *be* angry (like helping Jews in Nazi Germany: the Nazis would be angry, but we ought not to placate them). Here, as with lashing out at authority, we have to learn to control our emotions in regard to authority, whether they are 'attacking' emotions or 'placating' ones.

Armouring oneself   When we feel insecure one thing we can do is 'put on an act'. This is rather like putting on a suit of armour, or covering our soft insides with a shell like a crab. Sometimes this is sensible, when we have to be brave or get something done, or when it is not the right time to express our feelings. But often it is not sensible, because it puts us quite out of touch with the outside world, and in particular out of touch with other people. They have no chance of seeing what we are like, because we are too scared to show them. We pretend – to them and to ourselves – that we are brave, tough, confident, able to cope, etc., when in fact we may want help. Armouring oneself can be very dangerous, because it prevents us from sharing and communicating with other people.

Being 'respectable'   This is often a kind of armouring. We feel that we have to be 'good' in the way we have been brought up to be: for instance, we feel we have to be nice, clean, respectable, decent, not rude or common. Our self-respect or integrity may be tied up with this. We might feel ashamed of ourselves if we behaved otherwise – 'nice girls don't do that sort of thing', 'only common boys behave like that'. Whether this is sensible or not depends on *what we take being 'nice' or 'respectable' to be*. If it is just a set of conventions that do not do any good to other people, it may be silly; worse, it may be a way of cutting ourselves off from other people, keeping them at arm's length. If it is a genuine picture of 'niceness' in terms of other people's interests, then it may be very useful.

Having a secret life   Everybody has fantasies and day-dreams. We do not share our thoughts and feelings with other people all the time. Sometimes we give our 'secret life' particular forms: we keep diaries, write things on lavatory walls or make up poems that we will not show anybody. There is nothing particularly bad about this, but it is an open question as to what things to keep private and when. Again, it is a matter of controlling the emotion: often we feel unreasonably scared of sharing our 'secret life', although in a way we want to share it, if we could be sure people would not laugh at it.

Feeling you cannot communicate   Everyone feels this from time to time: there seem to be some things you cannot find words for, and some people who will 'never understand' (your parents, older people in general, the opposite sex). We may feel this too much, and think '*no one* can ever really understand *me*', and give up trying to share our feelings by talk: we imagine that we are the only people who have such feelings, which of course is not true. So we withdraw and give up. There is a sort of feeling like 'I am quite alone, we're all really quite alone', which has to be met by remembering that, in fact, there are other people with whom we can share if we try.

Feeling that life has no meaning   This is perhaps just a way of saying 'feeling depressed' or 'not really being able to enjoy anything': it has nothing to do with *life*, which is (partly) what we make it. Depression and a feeling of everything being pointless or without purpose is common to everybody, and then we need to withdraw from life, for a time anyway. But too much of it is a kind of illness, sometimes leading to suicide. Then we need help, which means that we need to recognize this feeling in good time. Sometimes it is attached to a particular misfortune – your girl or boy-friend leaves you, you fail an exam or something like that – but often it has nothing to do with anything particular. This too is a feeling that can be shared, and thus to some extent controlled.

ESCAPING SOMEWHERE ELSE

These patterns represent yet another way of coping – not by fighting or by withdrawing into your shell, but by *losing yourself* (so to speak) in something else: by surrendering yourself and your feelings to something outside yourself.

Idealizing people   Most of us feel the temptation to 'idealize' people, to see them as more powerful or glamorous or beautiful or important than they really are – almost, to see them as gods and goddesses. Falling in love is like this and so are certain kinds of religion, which make men into gods. The admiration or worship felt for Hitler, Mao Tse-tung, pop stars, the Queen, a war hero, perhaps one of your more glamorous or successful friends, or people on the TV or in films or books – the list is endless. We identify with these people and lose ourselves in admiration of them. This is harmless up to a point and in some circumstances. But (as the example of Hitler shows) we need to be able to be aware of it and control it. For it can be a way of giving up, and not leading our own life and making our own decisions.

Another world   Very similar is the desire to escape to 'another world', because we find this world too difficult, frightening or boring. We can do this via some kinds of religions, or we can do it by taking drugs, so that we give up this world and produce a new one in our own minds, one that is quite unreal but may be more attractive. Hippie groups and other people who opt out of society *may* be doing this, sometimes. Again, we need some picture of a better world, a state of affairs and a society preferable to what we have now; it all depends on how we use the picture. We may use it to inspire us, which is valuable, or we may use it as an escape, which may be inevitable for us when things get tough, but which is not ultimately satisfactory.

Following the crowd   We can 'lose ourselves', escape from our own problems, by joining a group or gang of people. This saves us from thinking for ourselves: we do and think just what everyone else does, like sheep. Of course there are many times when we cannot stand on our own feet, and need the support and reassurance of other people. Groups and gangs can be good in this way. Equally, there are times when we have to preserve our own identity and our own thoughts, when we have to resist the rest of the group. This may make us feel isolated, rejected, unwanted and generally insecure. We need sufficient control over our feelings as a member of the group, rather than just completely abandoning ourselves to it.

Following the fashion   You could describe fashion as a kind of extended group – 'what everyone is doing' (or wearing or buying). There are fashions not only in clothes, but also in cars, houses, records, songs, where to go for holidays, what sort of jobs to do, and even in moral and political opinions. People identify themselves with a fashion group: 'all teenagers nowadays do so-and-so'. Again, this can be harmless and amusing. But it can also be the sign of great insecurity, the feeling that unless you are 'in the fashion' you are not worth much, that nobody will admire or respect you unless you wear the 'right' clothes, live in the 'right' sort of house, like the 'right' records, and so on. This has to be resisted.

Seeking 'success'   We have put 'success' in inverted commas because we are talking about what our society counts as 'success' – that is, roughly, a lot of money, status, power, fame, being on the TV and so on. It is reasonable to want some 'success' in this sense – everyone wants to be recognized, to be thought important, by other people. We know perfectly well that 'success' in this sense does not necessarily bring either us or other people much happiness. Yet we are still sometimes tempted to pursue it very eagerly, as if it did. Here again, we feel that we only really exist and are 'real' or worth anything if we are 'successful'. We have to have the outward signs – a posh house, a big car – in order to persuade ourselves of our own worth. Genuine success depends on doing or being something that is genuinely worthwhile, even if it is not widely known and admired by other people.

Physical reassurance One of the simplest ways of making ourselves feel better, in the face of a harsh world, is to seek the simple pleasures. We may enjoy music, dancing, sex, a pint of beer, or whatever it may be. These give us simple physical reassurance, the feeling of pleasure that makes us feel 'real'. People who are too 'respectable' cannot do this, and suffer in consequence. At the same time, doing it too much is a sign of insecurity. Thus a person might spend long hours cuddling his girl-friend, or whole nights listening to music, or go on and on drinking: such a person is trying to comfort himself and lose himself altogether in these things. Again, it is all a question of the spirit in which it is done, and it can be done not in a spirit of pure enjoyment but as an escape. As with all the patterns, there is nothing right or wrong about it in itself – but it may be a sign that a person is emotionally insecure and needs help.

Part B
The Psychological Background

There is, perhaps, not all that much difficulty in working out a reasonably clear concept of authority, in the way described earlier. But that is not much use unless we also understand how we ourselves relate to that concept – how far we actually grasp it, what feelings we have about it and where those feelings come from. For authority is something we are all apt to feel strongly about, something that is liable to bring out our hang-ups. We need to understand ourselves much more clearly, and more deeply, if the concept is to be put into effective practice. How in fact *do* we (not *ought* we to) think and feel about authority?

We say 'how do *we* think about it', but who are the 'we'? It is important to realize that there are significant differences between different individuals and groups, and to appreciate what the differences are. Here we may be tempted to think that the important differences consist in whether a person or group is 'for' or 'against' authority in general, and certainly we can identify and distinguish two sorts of reactions.

CHAPTER 6
Two Attitudes

The first reaction we shall look at involves *identification* with authority. Here individuals (or the society as a whole) see themselves as the unquestionable representatives of a corpus of truths and values. They have the 'right answers', and their job is to pass these on to pupils so that they end up believing them and acting in accordance with them. Confident in this assumption, they welcome the power, authority, sanctions and disciplinary measures deemed necessary to put it into practice. The authority may be described or rationalized in different ways: Marxist ideology, a Christian way of life, British (French, etc.) culture and traditions, middle-class values or whatever. This posture is visible, in extreme forms, in totalitarian and authoritarian societies, although of course it is not confined to them.

The second reaction involves *rejection* of authority. Here individuals are in a state of reaction against whatever they take to be current authorities ('the establishment'). They do not regard their own beliefs and values as having priority over others, or as forming a firm and secure basis for education. They may indeed adopt some kind of relativist position in which the objectivity of truth and value is itself called into question or even denied. They are likely to favour non-hierarchical ideologies and some kind of egalitarianism (as it were, dismantling existing authority and dissipating it throughout society) along with certain interpretations of 'democracy' or 'participation'. They are likely to favour 'integration' and object to some practices as 'divisive' or 'elitist'. This posture is visible more often in liberal societies (the UK is a fair example).

It is fairly easy to see how each of these strays from the concept of education. On the one hand, the notion of education – indeed of learning itself – is connected with the logically basic notion of a *rational stance* towards the world. It is this stance that is primary: items claimed as truth or knowledge or worthwhile values derive their validity from that stance, from the primary concept of reasonable procedures, rather than vice versa. 'Right answers' cannot be the starting-point of education, since their rightness (if they are indeed right) can only be a function of the criteria of reason that justify them as right. This is perhaps most obvious in the case of moral education, where it is clear that no first-order set of values – no specific moral *content* – can be taken for granted. For such education, we have to rely on initiating pupils into a grasp of the rational procedures they can use to generate their own values. Objections to indoctrination, or the socialization of pupils into norms and practices that may well be questioned, rest ultimately on this point, as do legitimate demands under such headings as autonomy and critical thinking. Simply, the only authority an educator can ultimately recognize is the authority of reason itself, not of any particular or partisan ideology. On the other hand, to dismantle or reject authority in general, to react against the whole *concept* of 'right answers', is equally to stray from education, since the notions of reason, learning, knowledge, truth and hence of education itself are connected to that concept. Rational procedures (if we can get clear about them) do have authority, and educators can and must have authority insofar as they act as representatives of these procedures – for instance, as representatives and teachers of how to think reasonably about the physical world (science), about the past (history) and so on. Furthermore, educators need the practical or social authority necessary to transmit these procedures to their pupils – briefly, the authority and power necessary to enforce whatever discipline is required for education.

Although the distinction between these two attitudes is important, it may nevertheless be less important than a quite different distinction. We are familiar with the idea that *extremists* of both attitudes, like extremist Fascists and Communists, are apt to have a great deal in common. There is a distinction between extremism and moderation, fanaticism and common sense, which cuts across attitude to authority. The fact is that, somewhere in our minds, we feel *both* attitudes – that is why the pendulum swings so easily between them, between authoritarianism and chaos, totalitarianism and anarchy, a rigid and repressive use of authority and an abandonment of authority altogether. Hence, we should not be surprised if extremists start by being 'against' authority but then find themselves backing a very strong authority of their own – 'the party line', for instance, as against the old, hated authority of the Tsar and the aristocrats. The important thing, then, may be not whether we take sides – we are bound to feel both of them, more or less unconsciously – but how well we manage to *deal with* both sets of feelings.

Here is a quotation from an (unnamed) Nazi source, produced about 1938:

> Unquestioning obedience to his parents is the duty of every German child. But that is not enough. The authorities of the State are not to be challenged – in particular the laws and the Leader, Adolf Hitler, who is divinely appointed to rule us in every way. The police must be regarded as similarly appointed: it is not the business of the ordinary citizen to question them in any way. As for those who do – in particular the Jews, and all who seek to destroy the State – they deserve only our hate and our fury. We shall take revenge on them, be sure of that.

This sort of thing is present in all societies, more or less on or below the surface. Consider this edited report from the *Daily Mirror* (17 February 1987):

> 'By 1999 the urban war will be a permanent feature of everyday life in every city. . . . There will be guns and death on both sides.' This is not just a prediction. It is the earnest prayer of Britain's newest group of Fascist extremists – Nazis of the Left. They call themselves 'Class War'. They say they are Left-wing. But their aims and methods are no different from those of their Right-wing foes in National Front-style gangs – violence and chaos. When they achieve them, Class War will rise from the ashes to establish a new order – replacing the class system they despise.
>
> CW was founded two years ago by a handful of seasoned anarchists, and is now controlled by a secret politburo of 25 members.
>
> The movement has two 'newspapers' – *Class War* and *Angry*, which describes itself as the 'theoretical journal' of the party.
>
> Their 'theory' is stated as:
> - Being totally in favour of mugging the rich, shoplifting and burgling posh neighbourhoods, looting, assaulting the police and putting the boot in wherever we can.
> - Seeking to replace 'the State' with a series of 'self-policing' groups.

CHAPTER 7
Some Considerations from Research

We have looked at two general attitudes to authority and ended with an alarming and (deliberately) extreme example. If one asks normal children to say what they think about discipline and authority, much of what they say seems harmless and often sensible:

'I don't mind teachers telling me what to do if it's sensible.'

'It's funny, I never like being told what to do even if it's right.'

'I rather like being told what to do, it saves you having to think.'

'Why is it so good to be under discipline? Isn't self-discipline much better?'

'I'd always do what Miss X tells me, I just think she's marvellous.'

'My father's always bullied my big brother, he's just a wreck, I'm not going to be like that.'

'New kids ought to have more discipline, they don't know what's good for them.'

'When I have children I'm going to bring them up much more strictly.'

'You need discipline to keep you on the rails.'

'I don't mind discipline in playing football and that sort of thing. I'm keen on that. But in class – that's something different, it's boring.'

'The discipline in our school is far too strict, silly rules about uniform and things like that. What's it matter what you wear?'

But we can perhaps detect here – and in our own thinking – tendencies to extremism which we have to watch. It is not too far a step from the school bully to the member of the National Front who bullies racial minorities. We do not intend to suggest that 'normal' children are any more to be watched than 'normal' adults (there are plenty of horror stories to be told about both). But we desperately need to understand the roots of our feelings more deeply and in more detail. With this in mind, we and some colleagues interviewed several hundred people to find out what they thought about discipline and authority in schools – particularly about discipline, since this (we guessed) was the way in which the idea of authority impinged on them most directly. We divided up our respondents into four groups: (a) pupils of secondary school age, (b) parents of pupils at secondary schools, (c) teachers at secondary schools and (d) educational theorists and administrators. We then compiled a list of 20 questions, based on what seemed to be the most relevant features of discipline and authority. The questions were in three groups, as follows:

Conceptual clarity. Here we were concerned only with respondents' logical or conceptual grasp. These questions were (for reasons given earlier) perhaps the most important, but we did not usually ask them first; to do so, we found, tended to inhibit the respondents – as if they were being asked some sort of examination question. They asked whether the respondent grasped:

1. that discipline has to do with obedience?
2. that discipline has to do with obedience to legitimate authority as such (not for any old reason)?
3. the necessity ('value') of discipline in schools?
4. the necessity of discipline in life generally?
5. the need for rules backed by sanctions?
6. the need for the authority's legitimacy and power for *educational* purposes only?

Empirical fact. Here we were concerned with views on what was, or would under certain circumstances be, the case. The questions were:

7. Was discipline adequately understood in most schools?
8. Was it adequately enforced?
9. Was lack of enforcement because of lack of nerve and clarity, or other factors?
10. Would parents willingly contract to have it adequately enforced?
11. Would pupils willingly contract to have it adequately enforced?
12. Did pupils prefer existing disorder to more discipline?
13. Given the present state of the law, could discipline be adequately enforced?

Suggestions for improvement. Here we were concerned with some rather obvious suggestions, which they might or might not endorse. These were:

14. Should sanctions (of whatever kind) be sufficiently strong to ensure obedience?
15. Should teachers be trusted with the power to operate these sanctions?
16. Should there be a right of appeal by pupils against teachers, at least in some cases?
17. Should rules, contracts and sanctions be clearly and fully spelled out in schools?
18. Should the headteacher have more or less ultimate authority in matters of discipline?
19. Should some disciplinary powers be delegated to 'prefects' or other selected pupils?
20. Should discipline and authority be paid more attention to (in contrast with other educational objectives, e.g. academic or vocational knowledge and skill)?

We do not want here either to discuss fully the methodological problems of this sort of research or to present the research as having 'proved' anything in any 'scientific' way. Nevertheless, the results were interesting. We give in Table 1 the percentages of the people, in each of the four groups, who seemed to us (after lengthy interviews and discussions with each individual) to have entertained certain concepts and beliefs, and been willing to make certain prescriptions, in response to the questions above.

The most interesting thing about these responses was that pupils and parents (of course, with exceptions) were much more closely in touch with what we call an understanding and acceptance of discipline and authority than were many educational theorists – or even, it appears, some teachers! In the course of individual discussions it seemed that these concepts had largely disappeared from educational theory, or been misunderstood; whereas the pupils and parents, who of course had not been much or at all influenced by such theory, retained the approach we favour.

This research (we make no hard-and-fast claims for it) was at least sufficient for us to take seriously the question of why there seemed to be a good deal of opposition to notions of discipline and authority. To speak very generally, and in a sense to offer a conclusion in advance, we might say that one basic problem here is the *toleration of being separate*. Exercising authority and imposing sanctions involve *distancing* oneself from the other person in obvious

Table 1. *Specified responses (percentages)*

	a Pupils	*b Parents*	*c Teachers*	*d Educationalists*
Grasp of				
1. Discipline as obedience	73	81	56	24
2. Obedience to legitimate authority as such	55	73	31	16
3. Necessity for discipline in schools	91	98	85	53
4. Necessity for discipline in life generally	87	97	93	43
5. Need for rules backed by sanctions	91	99	71	34
6. Legitimate authority for education only	94	47	53	41
Belief that				
7. Discipline not adequately understood in schools	94	99	31	30
8. Discipline not adequately enforced in schools	90	99	65	41
9. Lack of enforcement chiefly due to lack of nerve and clarity	89	98	16	31
10. Parents would contract for enforcement	93	91	43	30
11. Pupils would contract for enforcement	83	73	38	27
12. Pupils did not prefer existing disorder	100	74	63	13
13. Discipline enforceable in existing state of law	91	98	31	30
Prescription that				
14. Sanctions be strong enough to ensure obedience	98	99	63	43
15. Teachers be trusted with power to operate these sanctions	81	80	56	37
16. There be right of appeal by pupils against teachers	100	98	90	98
17. Rules and contracts be clearly spelled out	98	82	63	52
18. Headteacher have ultimate authority subject to appeal	73	81	61	34
19. 'Prefects' be used for discipline	71	63	42	21
20. More attention paid to discipline and authority	92	99	78	56

ways. First, one is acting not as an equal or a friend, but as an impersonal authority and in a sense, therefore, not as a person at all, although one still remains a person when exercising this authority. Secondly, one is acting contrary to the desires of the other, i.e. preventing him or her from doing what he or she wants, perhaps creating suffering (by sanctions or the temporary withdrawal of affection) in fairly clear-cut ways. The problem is to continue valuing oneself when one has, to put it dramatically, made temporary enemies of other people.

One way of solving this problem is to see oneself as in touch with or sharing in some *external* source or sponsor of values. To take an extreme case, if a man sees himself as the prophet of the Lord, or as ordained by the Party to keep the revolution going, or whatever, he will be able to alienate himself from others because they are, so to speak, not his real spiritual home: his real home is with the Lord or the Party. Victorian parents – at least by repute – kept their nerve in respect of discipline by these means. They felt and believed that they were on the side of the right, not in the psychically weak sense that they believed in the rationality of what they enforced, but in the much stronger sense that they felt the right to have some sort of solid existence external to themselves – if not bound up with God, then at least more substantial than the apparently weak notion of 'being reasonable'.

Suppose now, as seems to be the case with many people, that this feeling is denied us. We now feel that we have no solid right to act as authorities at all. We cannot, as it were, be parents ourselves, because there is no solid parent with whom we can identify and be at home. The only alternative, it seems to us, is that we must all be children, all on the same level, sharing and enjoying things together without the need for rules, regulations, authorities, punishments and the whole apparatus of discipline. For this seems to offer us an alternative home, a tender-minded environment of 'mucking in' with our equals, in an atmosphere of care, concern and so forth. The idea is one of small children playing happily together, enjoying things for their own sake, being convivial. If (we feel) we can really make this work, then we need not be separate: there may be no external powers to join up with, but there will always be our friends, fellow-workers, comrades, chums, mates, etc.

Many contemporary phenomena may be quoted as instances of

this basic idea. We may mention, heterogeneously and in no sort of order, the vast quantity of left-wing or progressivist writing (Illich and so on) which stems either from Marxist fears of 'alienation' or from Rousseauesque feelings about the support and friendliness of 'nature'; the ethical relativism which has entered many philosophical circles; the phenomena of youth groups (the hippie communes are an example) that demonstrate the difficulty of child-like sharing in a clear form; and the passion for 'integration' and 'breaking down barriers', both in terms of distinctions between school subjects and in terms of differences between types of pupils (mixed ability, etc.), which itself shows a fear of separation or isolation in any form.

One important feature relevant to all this – whether it is best described as an aspect or a consequence of the fear of being separate – is the *absence of trust*. At the level of rationality, it is entirely plain that we have to trust people with authority and power in order to get certain jobs done efficiently, or done at all. The actual delegation of power, however, depends on the existence of some kind of trust, which in turn may be seen as dependent on the ability to tolerate some place or position in a hierarchy or structured system. This sort of place-filling is not only tolerable but positively inviting if, though only if, we accept and feel at home with the criteria by which the places are allotted. If we are not at home with them, we feel isolated and separated. To fill the place, and allow other people to fill their places, is thus ultimately dependent on the tolerance of separation. Either we feel reasonably secure in our separateness, and say things like, 'Oh, well, he is the teacher (policeman, minister, etc.) after all', 'She's a reliable sort, let her get on with the job', and so on, or we do not feel secure, and try to defeat our isolation by joining other groups.

Plato and a long line of later thinkers believed that it was possible and desirable to impose authority from above, and to make such imposition permanently effective. There are at least some doubts about its desirability. Yet even if it was desirable, the psychic roots of the opposition – if our suggestions are at all near the mark – cast even more doubt on its possibility. One might, indeed, imagine a society (one version could resemble Orwell's *Nineteen Eighty-Four*) in which authority was successfully imposed by sufficient psychic control. Yet even the permanence of this is questionable, and for nearly all actual societies as they are today the possibility is an academic one. This means that the only way forward, especially for our own and similar societies, must be by the achieving of greater *understanding* of discipline and authority. From there comes the emotional and practical acceptance of them.

There are reasons why such understanding and acceptance must *begin*, at least, with greater conceptual clarity. It might be supposed, as an alternative, that 'common sense' or experience will eventually do the trick: perhaps things will eventually both be and seem so bad to ordinary people that there will be a swing of the pendulum, a backlash in favour of authority. The trouble with this is that such swings may be no more than the takeover of one fear by another. The dread of chaos, rather than separation, may take its turn to invade the ego and produce certain kinds of arrangements – an obsessive puritanism, a dictator or whatever. But greater rationality can only emerge if we *learn* from these swings. Characteristically, neither individuals nor societies return to 'common sense' *simply* under the pressure of dramatic events. Such pressure is much more likely to drive them further in the direction of the nonsensical and the doctrinaire.

To put things fairly bluntly, and without the benefit of more sophisticated sociological or psychoanalytic theory, it is as if most of us still thought of authority in the way that members of ancient societies or very young children might think of it – not as a necessary piece of equipment to get certain things done, but in a semi-magical way (rather as one might believe in blue blood or the divine right of kings). Many of our respondents were either in favour of authority in this sense, or against it; most were perhaps ambivalent towards it. Specifically in reference to the teacher's authority, there was clearly a feeling that teachers either should or should not be – to put it dramatically – invested with some sort of numinous power calling for 'respect', if not awe. Rather like priests, they were seen either as having this power (and therefore they ought not to be jostled, sworn at or treated as ordinary human beings), or as pretenders, 'no better than we are' (and therefore they ought to be stripped of all power).

However fanciful this may seem, it at least fits the numerous remarks made by interviewees that had no connection with *rational* authority at all – the constant references to sex, bad language, dress and so forth. We do not say that these features are unimportant if, as may well be the case, they are connected in the *pupils'* minds with the power of teachers; just as, although we know that monarchs excrete, simple-minded people might lose respect for the crown if they actually saw them doing so. Such is the power of fantasy or magic. Rational discipline and authority, of course, depend on understanding the point of *entitlement*, of entrusting certain people with certain delimited powers to do a certain job. This is a matter of rules and adherence to rules, not of being swayed by charisma.

For fairly obvious social reasons, which must presumably include at least the rise in power (together with increased leisure, money and articulateness) of a working class now largely alienated from traditional authorities, and perhaps also the natural decay in acceptance of such authority-sponsoring metaphysics as Christianity, respect for visible holders of authority has declined over the past four or five decades (perhaps for longer) – we mean for actual teachers, police officers, politicians, parents, priests and so forth. But it has not been replaced by respect for rational authority. That seems to be too sophisticated a concept, or rather too impersonal a practice, for our feelings to accept wholeheartedly. It is *not* the case that, for instance, respect for the law has increased as respect for judges and police officers has diminished, nor that respect for business contracts has grown as fear of bosses has declined, nor that respect for the impersonal rules required to run schools has become greater as the teacher has come to be held in less awe.

All this may be more or less common ground, but it presents a basic problem that may be roughly stated thus: given people as they are – that is, apparently incapable of firmly grasping and using the notion of rational authority – should we (a) try to *educate* them so that they can obtain such a grasp, or (b) give rational authority up as a bad job, and reinforce some kind of non-rational authority? The former move will, of course, naturally appeal to those of a tender-minded and (roughly) 'liberal' disposition; the latter, to those who are more tough-minded, and are prepared to see 'law and order' flourish at almost any cost. In the wider political field, a broad distinction may be drawn between those who look for salvation in terms of more democracy, participation, autonomy and so forth on the one hand, and those who feel that a society's only hope may lie in a strong man, a hard line, or even dictatorship. It is a regrettable symptom of our own intellectual incompetence that the words 'discipline' and 'authority' have come to be associated – wrongly, as we have seen – almost exclusively with the latter.

The most important thing here is to see the lunacy of taking sides. Returning to our question, we can see that there must be at least *some* people who have a proper grasp of the concepts, some 'educated' group, some set of individuals who will be able to transmit their understanding to others or, insofar as that proves impossible, able to make the right judgements on others' behalf. So the desirability of more education about discipline is clear enough. But we can also see that meanwhile the wheels have to be kept turning; that, even if only in order to be *able to educate* people in discipline, our schools (and indeed our society) must be reasonably trouble-free; that we must have order and obedience in the first place if our 'liberal' aims are to be fulfilled. Moreover, there will also always be some people – very young children, psychopaths and so on – who cannot or will not, however hard we try, grasp the necessary concepts. Not everything can, in practice, be achieved by education.

Teachers here are in a peculiar, indeed virtually a unique, position, for they have the dual role of education and keeping order. Most other people in positions of authority are concerned only with keeping order – that is, they have to ensure that certain things get done, that certain rules are obeyed. It is not their job, or not primarily their job, to *teach* anybody anything. In the minds of many teachers, it appears, there is a conflict between education and keeping order. It is as if 'educating' or 'teaching' *meant*, for them, something that was essentially 'non-authoritarian', involving only the children's interest, or their willing participation. Hence the term 'discipline' comes to stand (wrongly) for something rather sophisticated and remote from the idea of obedience to authority in a task-like situation; to stand, perhaps, for what might be meant by 'self-discipline' or even something like 'being genuinely absorbed in some activity' or 'wanting to learn'. (Something of the same role-conflict may perhaps be observed in social workers and others.)

But it is certain that *teachers*, at least, *must* be clear about authority, for they are the people who have the task of educating the coming generation in that respect. Whatever may be gained by educating people to understand and practise rational authority can only be gained via teachers. The obvious first step, then, must be the re-education of teachers. We are not saying here that we should delay other steps perhaps equally obvious: by 'first' we mean that it has a clear logical priority, that it is a step that we quite evidently *must* take, whatever else we do. Nor, of course, are we saying that we need not bother to educate *other* people – parents, educational administrators, and so on – in this respect, but that the natural priority lies in teachers.

What would this first step consist of? Initially we might want to say that professionalization of teachers should include more clarification of concepts. That is philosophy, provided that 'philosophy' is used in the right way: to refer to a study and a context of communication in which the meanings of words are properly understood, in which no particular partisan 'line' is taken about educational or other issues, and where the prejudices and fantasies of those taking part are diminished by an increase in their clarity and common sense. All this has to be stressed, because a good deal of what is called 'philosophy of education', particularly where discipline is concerned, simply reinforces or sophisticates certain fantasies. This vice is, of course, common to all of us; we are not here trying to pass arrogant comments on the writing of other authors. Our point is simply that unless a professional philosophy *does* give us clarity and diminish our fantasies, it is of no use and may even be harmful.

This does not mean that teachers, and especially student-teachers, should spend less time in hard thinking and more time in what some quaintly describe as 'practical' training. There is a fashion, stemming perhaps partly from a disenchantment with the usual content of educational theory, for laying more stress on this 'practical' side, but this in itself will not and cannot help the teachers to retain and enlarge their common sense and conceptual competence. They need many hours of argument and conceptual discussion, in which a tough-minded accuracy about the meanings of words may help to defend them against prejudice. Without this, we have little chance of remaining level-headed in a world of constantly changing educational fashion and pressure.

There is one respect in which 'practical' training may be useful here. Many people, particularly those without experience of responsibility and organization, will defend themselves and their ideas about discipline in almost any context of discussion or argument. Such people need to be shown, in as 'real' and vivid a way as possible, the kind of disasters that can follow from their ideas. Limited experience in schools – a term's teaching practice, for instance – is often not much use here: they are thereby made accustomed to a system which is itself largely fantasy-based, and in which the disasters of fantasy are not sufficiently apparent. But put a person in charge of (say) a mountaineering party in which people may fall to their deaths, of a business enterprise in which people may go broke, of a sailing-ship in which people may drown, and the pay-off resulting from lack of discipline becomes more immediately apparent than it usually is in schools. Common sense breaks through more easily when the disasters and advantages are easily visible.

It also seems important that all teachers should be helped to recognize fantasy for what it is in some rather more direct way. Although comparatively little work has been done in this field – at least, not in specific reference to education – most of the major fantasies connected with education are tolerably clear, and could easily be categorized: it would be almost as easy to identify these in student-teachers and others. Most competent teacher-educators, in fact, who take the trouble to know their pupils as people, have a pretty good idea of what sorts of fantasies are at work with what pupils. Much is, no doubt, to be learned from clinical psychiatrists and from whatever reasonable forms of group therapy, counselling or group dynamics may commend themselves.

Some of the most striking results of interviews relate to the notion of control (rather than that of discipline, although there are connections). To many respondents, as we had anticipated, discipline more or less *meant* control. Although, in fact, discipline refers to only one way of maintaining control or social order, we felt it worthwhile to find out something about views on control.

Hardly anybody thought that pupils ought not in principle to be controlled, but there was a considerable difference in their views on the *extent* and *methods* of control. Teachers and administrators were much more diffident than parents and (perhaps surprisingly) pupils about both the extent and the methods. Particularly remarkable is the fact that very many parents, and not a few pupils, felt not only that the school authorities should exercise control over behaviour – a point on which they were more or less in line with the teachers and administrators, although much more tough-minded about it – but also that the authorities should exercise more control over the pupils' *work*, not only in school hours but also outside the school. The enforcement of homework was the clearest issue here.

They were also much more prepared to countenance tough-minded methods of control. Some, perhaps ignorant of legal and other facts of life, regarded teachers as feeble or cowardly for not actually applying these methods. 'If you can't clobber him yourself, just you tell me what he's done and I'll make sure he doesn't do it again' was a common idea, particularly among fathers. They had at least a firm grasp of the idea that teachers should be respected and obeyed, even if they lacked something of the idea of impersonal obedience to authority. Teachers and administrators, by contrast, felt that control was chiefly a matter of being 'stimulating' or 'interesting' (except with regard to certain groups of extremely difficult pupils), that it was somehow *their fault* if they could not interest the pupils in learning and hence control them. They felt themselves to be not representatives of impersonal authority but either possessing or failing to possess the requisite techniques or charisma. This was particularly and perhaps unsurprisingly true of younger teachers and those who had been influenced by recent educational theory.

An interesting point here is that both parents and pupils (more obviously, perhaps, pupils) often did *not*, in their actual behaviour, live up to their ideas. Everyone is familiar with the parent who is possessive about his or her own child ('Don't you lay a hand on my Johnny'), and disobedient or non-respectful pupils are commonplace. The majority of our interviewees in these categories said that they had, in fact, behaved thus on some occasions. We did our best, therefore, in the course of the conversations to make sure that their expressed views were actually sincere, and found not only that they were, but that the subjects recognized the partisan or egocentric feelings that governed them and others on such occasions and, partly for that very reason, thought control to be all the more important. The general message was, 'Well, of course you get carried away when it's *you* (your child), you don't think about the rules. But somebody has to keep order and make sure people stay in line. I'd vote for that straight away.'

We hence have the rather remarkable fact that the *consumers* – the parents and pupils – are not only willing but anxious, when properly talked to, to have some adequate method of control and to give teachers the necessary powers. The teachers and educational-ists themselves seemed, in general, to be much more uncertain about it, even though they often quoted what they supposed to be the consumers' views in defence of their own uncertainty ('the parents wouldn't stand for it', 'you can't treat pupils like that nowadays', and so on). With some hesitancy, we might account for this by suggesting that, for the kind of tender-minded and idealistic liberals of whom teachers and (still more) educators are largely representative, the mere idea of actually *holding power* produced serious feelings of guilt. Parents, and perhaps also pupils, lacked this disadvantage. They also had the additional advantage of seeing more clearly what naked power is actually like, and why clear-cut and tough-minded forms of control are absolutely necessary to prevent abuse of it. (Anyone who has brought up a family of normal, lively children finds it much more difficult to sustain an idealistic liberalism *all* the time.)

That the notions of guilt and repressed aggression are not out of place here may be suggested by some of the replies from teachers, which indicate a degree of conflict and compulsion far greater than one might casually suppose. 'If the only way you could, in practice, stop one child bullying and torturing another was to make him frightened of you and your power, would you make him fright-ened?' 'Oh no, I couldn't do that, you shouldn't make anyone frightened, it's wrong.' 'But if that were the only way – I mean, if you didn't have time to do it by love and influence and the force of example?' 'Well, I just couldn't, I just couldn't live with myself if I did.' 'But doesn't bullying make you very angry?' 'Very, but that's all the more reason to control myself.' 'So you'd just let the bullying go on?' 'Well, I suppose I'd have to. Perhaps I could tell the little child to keep out of the big one's way.'

Something of the difference between what is felt by at least some teachers and what is felt by other people in authority emerged fairly clearly in a short study (made in conjunction with this particular project) of a school cruise. (Perhaps we should say in advance that in our judgement, for what it is worth, these cruises are admirable institutions for all sorts of reasons, and this cruise may well have been atypical.) The teachers who went with the pupils exercised far less control over them than the ship's officers; not because they had less power or for any other reason, but plainly because the whole *exercise* of authority did not come so naturally to them, and because they lacked confidence in themselves as holders of authority. The officers, who treated the children with much more firmness and even severity, became objects of respect – and, rather strikingly, affection and attachment – much more quickly than the teachers (who, in most cases, were not originally known to the children any more than the officers were). We do not imply any general praise of naval officers at the expense of the teaching profession, but it was clear that they had the immense advantage of working within a clear and properly enforced disciplinary structure. It is significant that their authority was of more value, even for the purposes of education in this context, than that which the teachers vaguely attempted to wield.

This may generate the suggestion that most of the problem may stem from the fact that teachers do not *have* to control the pupils, so that they are not forced into exercising authority by sheer necessity, they are not *encouraged* to do so effectively by colleagues or other educationalists and they are not *enabled* to do so by the existence of a proper disciplinary structure that gives them an adequate backing. If any fault lies with the teachers, it is that they are either not clear-headed enough, or not courageous enough, to demand the control they clearly ought to have. In this respect, as perhaps in some others, teachers appear as an oppressed and under-privileged class, deferentially accepting what is thought to be (but is not) current public opinion about their proper powers and scope.

Some of the trouble lies simply in the common inability to imagine 'the system' as anything radically other than it actually is. In many of our conversations we raised the possibility that teachers in state schools might have something of the independence and control enjoyed by, for instance, at least some members of staff in independent boarding schools. The very idea seemed to some of them so novel as to be virtually incomprehensible: it was as if we had offered them the vision of a totally new world. The newness was, in general, alarming for most, though attractive for many; they responded to the possibility of power or influence in predictable ways. The majority fell back on reasons why this would, in any case, be impossible except under the peculiar conditions that apply to the independent boarding schools: 'you can only do that if they're boarders', 'the parents have chosen to send them there, ordinary parents wouldn't stand for it', 'they're all upper-middle-class pupils, it wouldn't work with the rest', and so on. Whether or not any of these reasons actually have force, they were not deployed for their intrinsic merits. As the teachers saw it, 'the system' was what it was, and somehow there must be reasons for it, or the conflict between what is and what might be would seem intolerable.

In all this, it is worth repeating, the teachers are much to be pitied rather than blamed. This is not so for the administrators. They do not have to face large classes of undisciplined children every day, without any semblance of power or effective means of control. They are free to exercise their ideas as committee members, politicians or general commentators on education. In imposing these ideas on those who do the actual work, however, they are much at fault. All of us have our fantasies, but those of us who are in positions of intellectual influence ought to take particular care to keep them to ourselves.

Educationalists and administrators have rarely been in positions requiring *disciplinary* control – that is, as we have seen, control over small groups in task-like situations. The most common case of such experience for older (male) politicians was some kind of military service. However, the structure and back-up for authority was so strong and clear, in that particular case, that they were perhaps not brought up sharply against disciplinary *problems* or, if they were, the mechanisms for resolving those problems were simple and effective. This is unlike the cases of, say, being in charge of a recalcitrant gang of labourers, a youth leader or any similar role where the powers and effectiveness of authority are less obvious. It is indeed rather hard to find even moderately close analogies with the teacher's role because the need for discipline is unusually great and its enforceability unusually small. Senior army officers who have successfully controlled large forces in desert warfare have been known to be reduced to rubble when trying to control the Fifth Form. From this point of view, one very important obstacle to improvement is simply that the present state of affairs is regarded as acceptable. Children are often no longer expected to obey, attend and remain reasonably silent: perhaps 'reasonably' is construed well below the level of what reason in fact demands. An 'acceptable noise level', for instance, is often one in which the teacher has to make a special effort to be heard. Any teacher who actually wants to *teach*, of course, will naturally often want virtually *no* noise and virtually *total* attention. That will be the proper norm, even if it is sometimes or even often broken – and, when it is broken, something has gone wrong. But this is no longer widely regarded as a norm. On the contrary, it is regarded, in some schools, as some sort of airy-fairy ideal, impossible of fulfilment by any means at all. However, other schools show clearly that it can be done.

Another obstacle is the peculiar deference and insecurity that seem to run widely through the education system. In most independent schools the relationship between the head and his or her official superiors (the governing body) is far less fraught than in most state schools. Teachers in the public sector are far more worried about their jobs, their public image, and their relationships with the local authority and with parents than are their independent counterparts. Many reasons contribute to this, but one fairly obvious to anyone who has had adequate experience of both sectors is (roughly) that most teachers in the state system feel themselves to be more vulnerable, less powerful, less confident and less connected to that upper-middle-class and/or upper-class world, among the chief characteristics of which is supposed, at least, to be a certain style of self-confidence (often criticized, not always unjustly, as arrogance or superciliousness). They do not feel themselves to be professionals of the same standing as (for instance) the barrister or the doctor.

This deference prevents them from even envisaging, let alone operating, the kind of 'staging' or stage-setting necessary for the deployment of autonomous power (which is very obvious in traditional independent schools, where it may require considerable nerve for parents even to question the school's power). Few schools are so constructed as to reinforce the hierarchical potency of headteachers, or to demonstrate to the outside world that the school is a world of its own with its own values, powers and authority.

With many respondents we discussed, albeit rather vaguely, widespread forms of juvenile or semi-juvenile delinquency, including, for instance, theft, arson, forms of violence, damage to property, mugging and bullying, but excluding the (comparatively) rare offences of murder, rape or extreme forms of assault. We do not suggest that these latter require a type of treatment that is, at all points, logically different from that required by the former. But we confined ourselves to the former chiefly because one or other of such forms of misbehaviour was within the experience of our respondents.

Undoubtedly the most striking fact here was that the vast majority of our respondents seemed to echo or represent neither what might be thought of (at least if one judges by what appears in the national press) as current *opinion* on these matters, nor what seems to be our society's current *practice* in dealing with them. Current opinion, or those parts of it that publicity is most apt to highlight, includes at least two types of reaction. These are: first, a generalized view of such behaviour as a 'social product' (arising from bad homes, insufficient space for games playing, healthy aggression, or whatever), to be dealt with by some kind of sociological method rather than by the normal application of rules and punishments; and secondly, a sharply retributive reaction (birch them, put them in the stocks, send more of them to prison, etc.). Current practice, it seems, is incapable of solving the problems by any method. Fines are increased, trouble is avoided by banning attendance at football matches and vast sums of money are spent on prevention and protection ('vandal-proofing' whatever has to be protected), but nothing very effective is done.

Most of our respondents took a different view of the matter. They were clear that clear rules and punishments had to be laid down, and properly publicized, for all such offences; the punishments had to be effective as deterrents – that is, sufficiently unpleasant to prevent the misdoers from engaging in such behaviour; restitutive justice should be enforced by making the offenders pay back, in terms of time and effort, for the damage or unpleasantness they had inflicted. Perhaps even more importantly, they mostly believed that some *person* or group of people had to be entrusted with sufficient on-the-spot power to ensure that this apparatus was actually effective. It was widely believed that if the police, the family, the probation officers and (ultimately) the magistrates were as ineffective as they seemed to be, then for those under school age at least the authority should reside in the school – that is, in the headteacher and whatever other teachers had responsibility for the particular offender.

In some (if few) schools, of course, this is *de facto* the case. If a pupil is detected in, say, the offence of causing damage to property, then – whether or not he or she comes up before the courts – the headteacher will in fact ensure that the pupil has clearly understood beforehand that such behaviour counts as an offence, is sharply deterred from doing it again, and makes good the damage. In other words, the school does take on responsibility, and has the power to enforce it, for such occurrences. This responsibility and power are by no means entirely confined to the independent boarding schools. There appears to be no reason, other than the traditional impotence of many schools in our society, why all schools should not do this job. As the replies show, there is little doubt that most parents would wish it. Doubts about it are found mostly among educational theorists and administrators.

Here again an external observer, looking at current practice, might suppose that there was general acceptance of some view to the effect that it should be *nobody's* job to ensure that (for example) pupils behaved properly on school coaches, did not vandalize telephone kiosks after school hours and so on. It is as if, knowing that the police could not be everywhere, we vaguely hoped that parents or the home would improve the situation, but did not feel strongly enough about it to empower any authority actually to deal with it. Even when railway carriages are almost totally destroyed, or bus drivers refuse to transport hooligans, we seem to think – or so, at least, it appears – that nothing much can be done. That is, indeed, the practice. The notion that parents, teachers, pupils and (we dare say) the public at large, do not *want* to empower an authority to deal with it is, according to our findings at least, demonstrably false. They do want to, and in default, at least, of any other kind of 'local disciplinarian' (so to speak) they are anxious for teachers to take on the job.

In our view, what is most alarming is not the actual 'misbehaviour' of pupils in or out of school, the vandalism prevalent in many neighbourhoods, the hooliganism at football matches and so forth. These and similar phenomena are, it seems to us, entirely predictable in the absence of clear and adequate control. *Of course* pupils without discipline will behave in this way; *of course* teenagers, full of energy and excitement, will start fights and smash things up. It is ridiculous to say that they are in no sense to blame, being merely the products of society. Yet it is almost equally absurd to say that they are in every sense to blame, since that implies some awareness on their part of clear and adequate rules that they deliberately break – though often there are no clear and adequate rules. It is rather that the very concepts of blame, responsibility, rule-breaking and so on have, in many areas of behaviour, simply not been introduced into their lives. What precisely (for instance) are they allowed to do on football terraces, and what are they not allowed to do? How are these approved and disapproved items of behaviour publicized, if at all, and does anyone make it *clear* to them? What sanctions are made clear to them, attached to what items? What measures are taken to identify rule-breakers – are the cameras on them, are there people in authority taking notes and names? Since the answers to all these questions are either negative or at best unclear, it is not surprising that they have no more than a vague idea of 'what they can get away with'.

It is important to appreciate that the desired moves may be made without getting into complicated arguments about 'values' or 'ideology'. The minimal rules required for serious learning to go on in schools and for pupils in schools to be tolerably happy, or at least immune from non-controversial dangers, are pretty obvious and hardly in dispute. We *know* that pupils should turn up on time, pay attention to the teacher, do their homework, not bully each other, not vandalize property and so on. These are not items in a particular 'ideology' but necessary conditions for any serious institution of learning. Others, no doubt, are more disputable: for instance, the merits and demerits of school uniforms, organized games, the use of 'bad language', long hair and many other things may be argued about. But these arguments can wait until we have established the necessary minimum.

Our advice would be that those parties to the business of education – whether parents, teachers, pupils or educationalists – who do in fact feel that something should be done should *first* canvass opinion in the case of their particular school. Is it, in fact, true that the school's parents are content with the present position? Would they (as our own survey suggests that they might) actually prefer something different? It would be clear on the basis of such an enquiry – which is not too difficult to carry out in the case of a single school – just what the demand or consensus is. If, as is likely, some clear idea is gained of what sort of changes would be necessary, there is then every reason in the world to press for such changes by whatever methods seem appropriate.

We also discussed whether things were worse now than they used to be. We have phrased this question as vaguely as possible, precisely in order to remind the reader that there will be various answers, depending on what *things* are supposed now to be worse or better and in what *respects*, compared with *when* in the past. A complete survey of the possible and relevant options is impossible here but, as far as discipline goes, three points may be worth making.

First, we have no doubt that the *concept* of authority and discipline in educational contexts, compared with the situation in the UK of, say, 30 years ago, has in fact sunk further below the surface. Indeed it has in some degree passed out of the immediately conscious grasp of many people – that is, it is disappearing or has to some extent disappeared. Evidence for this cannot, of course, be anything like conclusive from our particular sample. Nevertheless, it is certainly highly suggestive that older respondents were conceptually clearer than younger ones, that those less directly concerned with education were clearer than those more directly concerned and that the concept still flourished in some (perhaps nearly all) non-educational contexts (e.g. in questions about ships, the army and other task-like situations) in the minds of those who had dispensed with it in educational contexts.

Secondly, the *practice* of discipline does not lend itself to any reliable generalizations. Certainly it is plausible to say (on grounds not connected with our own research) that children in schools 30 years ago were more rigidly *controlled*; it may even be likely that they were more *obedient*, that is, more obedient to authority. Being well-disciplined involves, as we have seen, obeying authorities as authorities and not as anything else, and it seems extremely doubtful whether pupils in past ages grasped this idea any more firmly than pupils nowadays. Perhaps, indeed, they grasped it less firmly. It is entirely possible that their obedience was due to other factors (most obviously, fear of punishment or some kind of respect for 'charismatic' authority), and that nothing very much has changed except a diminution of that fear, with a corresponding lack of control. That would, indeed, be our guess, a guess to some extent supported by remarks made by older respondents about their own reasons for obedience when they were pupils. Clearly no reliable judgements can be made here, nor (since we cannot now with any certainty enter the minds of pupils of 30 years ago) is it easy to see how any such judgements ever could be made.

Thirdly, although (as has been suggested) *control* may now be much worse, it is not entirely clear that either the concept or the practice of restitutive justice are in any worse a state. In the past, although retributive justice (with its usual connotations of painful punishment rather than recompense) no doubt flourished more, so that in *this* sense there would be both a stronger theory and practice of 'paying back', there is no very obvious evidence that retribution as straightforward recompense was more favoured than it is now.

This general picture may be true of much contemporary behaviour in our society over a wider spectrum. The diminution of control and obedience to authority (whether or not as authority, and whether or not for the right reasons) is a different matter from the rejection of rational and rationally desirable ends and procedures. One might suspect, indeed, that the grasp that people have of these latter – the degree to which their thought and action are governed by reason – may remain, in a broad way, comparatively constant. Perhaps one fantasy simply replaces another, or becomes uppermost at a particular time. What many of us are accustomed to regard as security, law and order, etc. may be founded on nothing more than a coincidence of (bad) reasons with ends or states of affairs that happen to be desirable.

This does not mean, of course, that control is unimportant. We are concerned (indeed as educators we are particularly or perhaps uniquely concerned) with the advancement of understanding, with people doing things for the right reasons. We are also concerned simply that the right or necessary things should *get done*, that trouble should be avoided, contracts kept, crime prevented and so on. These states of affairs are good in their own right, and remain of paramount importance even if the reasons for which people act in respect of them are demonstrably absurd. The mere rejection of particular versions or images of non-rational authority, far from giving any comfort to those of broadly liberal persuasion, should more properly alarm them. If such rejection does not at once give place to the acceptance of a rational authority, and if the rejection also involves the disappearance of control, we simply find ourselves fighting hot or cold wars – a grave situation in which (if we survive at all) the nature of things inevitably imposes a harsher and more tyrannical authority even than the one we originally rejected.

We also discussed the question of why those teachers who understood discipline did not enforce it. There are various answers to this, but we may start with one possibility that is certainly *not* the, or even an, answer. Their failure to enforce it was *not* the result of carelessness, lack of feeling or any weakness of will. On the contrary, nearly all the teachers we spoke to were extremely upset, and often very bitter, about the absence of enforcement. They certainly *cared* enough about it. As we have seen, the correlation between those interviewees who understood the concept and those who saw its necessity and value was very high – almost all those who realized what discipline was also realized its importance. Why then did they not enforce it?

We have here to distinguish between headteachers (together with those who held offices that had quasi-political or public relations aspects – some deputy heads, for instance) and ordinary classteachers. The former group saw their jobs in essentially political or public relations terms. Their chief aim was not so much that discipline should be enforced, justice done and authority clearly perceived, but rather that their school – considered as a political entity – should not fall foul of any powerful external body (in particular parents and local authorities, but also the press), and if possible acquire or retain a good reputation. Their chief anxiety, conversely, was that the *appearance* of something bad (violence, nasty remarks in the press, parental disapproval, etc.) might upset the precarious stability of their position.

In saying this, we do not suggest that all these headteachers were weak-kneed or had an eye to the main political chance. It was clear from many conversations that many of them would ('under ideal conditions', as was commonly said) have run properly disciplined and well-organized schools. The point was rather that they simply did not have the power, and with the absence of power, there rapidly ensued an absence of nerve to do things that might have been within even their slender powers. They felt, with justice, that under modern conditions, a headteacher simply could not *survive* – at least psychologically, even if he or she retained the job – if there was more than a minimal amount of 'trouble'. It was as if they felt themselves to be sitting on a volcano, trying to keep the lid on. Hence, as is virtually inevitable for those in political positions, most of their energies were devoted to avoiding such 'trouble', to keeping things going by any available methods.

Much the same is true of the class-teachers, except that they were frightened of their position and repute *vis-à-vis* the head. They could not, in general, rely upon the head to back them up with sufficient firmness in cases of indiscipline, and they themselves preferred to skate over such cases rather than bring them to the head's attention. They were themselves aware that the headteacher lacked sufficient powers to do very much about it, and relied on the usual mixture of coaxing, persuading, cajoling, bribing or simply overlooking pupils who caused trouble, while expecting the teachers to do the same. 'I don't want to be a trouble-maker' was, in one form or another, a common thought, or, 'after all, what can we do when it comes to the crunch?'

Although some teachers stood out firmly in favour of some particular kind of sanction (corporal punishment, for instance) the majority appreciated that – other things being more or less equal – the *type* of sanctions mattered much less than their *efficacy*. 'The only point is, they must learn who is in charge' was a common idea, as was 'whatever we do, we have to make it stick'.

Most realized (surely correctly) that *if* it was true, and seen by the pupils to be true, that the school authorities – whether in the person of the headteacher or individual teachers – *did* have the power to make their orders stick, then cases of indiscipline would greatly diminish. It was, as they saw, establishing this point of principle, i.e. 'who is in charge', that counted for practically everything. This is little to do with what sanctions are actually employed, or how often, but a great deal to do with the nerve and confidence of those deploying them. Various suggestions were made: that the school should simply stop educating the pupil until he or she had learned to obey and accept authority; that some rapid shock treatment (corporal punishment or something of that kind) be administered until it worked; that persistent offenders should be publicly declared unemployable; that they should be removed from the school altogether; that they should be kept in detention indefinitely, and so on. But most subjects held less strong views about the type of sanctions than about their effectiveness in showing 'who is in charge'.

Finally, the question may be raised, not of whether this movement towards the establishing of rational authority and contractual clarity *ought* to be made – that seems to us beyond dispute – but of whether it is in fact *likely* to be made. Here we entertain grave doubts. In some parts of the world, where disciplinary conditions are extremely bad, there have nevertheless been few attempts to reinstate rational authority. Continued chaos seems to be preferred, and dissatisfied individuals simply move out (if they can) of the chaotic context. The alternative to reinstating rational authority is a well-known phenomenon: things eventually get so bad all round (not only in schools) that some powerful authority, of a charismatic and non-rational kind, emerges with enough support to take over. Unable to grasp (let alone realize in practice) the notion of rational authority, people then cling to the representatives of some specific ideology – usually of a puritanical kind – who will at least 'maintain law and order'. This in turn is doomed to perish, since (because it is non-rational) it carries with it particular values that will, sooner or later, come under attack. And so the wheels turn.

The kind of non-rational authority liable to take over is familiar to us. It is based on a confused but potent picture of the 'good' pupil, 'good' being construed not at all or not only in terms of rational criteria but in terms of a particular life-style. In this vein, the 'good' pupil is perhaps clean and tidy, does not use 'bad language', does not criticize his or her elders, is in uniform, does not express sexual or aggressive feelings in any way alarming to adults, and so on. Still less rational pictures might include some idea of racial or social class purity, an element of male dominance, strict censorship of 'corrupting' literature and the visual arts, and so on. That is the price we may pay if we cannot develop enough clarity and sophistication to make authority work in the right way.

We are not optimistic about the future, if only because of certain obvious truths. The ego and the forces maintaining rationality are, even in the most sophisticated of us, fragile when compared to those of the irrational and the unconscious mind, sparked off and sustained as they are by the pushes and pulls of 'society' and ideology. The virtues of common sense may not be strong enough to survive.

Already there are signs of a general loss of confidence in public institutions of all kinds, and too many people may simply choose to opt out. Already there are schools where conditions are such that sensible and well-educated parents say to their children something like: 'Look, you have to sit through this chaos, it's the law; but when you come out at four o'clock perhaps we can teach you something worth learning. Meanwhile just try to survive.' Others, of course, try to rake up the money to send their children to schools where more rational standards might prevail.

On the other hand, there are some grounds for optimism. The clarity and rationality required do not, at least for the respondents in our own survey, lie too far below the surface. In the case of parents at least, whose jobs are not at stake and who are not too deeply enmeshed in the system to give up all hope of bringing about change, many respondents seemed willing to take the action required. Perhaps there is still time for us to come to our senses. It would, of course, be extremely helpful if educational theorists, politicians, researchers and administrators were to assist this process, and encourage the thinking of parents and teachers along the lines of reason; but that may be too much to hope for. Educational research, theory and administration are largely self-sustaining industries, and have long since severed many of their links with truth and rationality. It may even be fairer to say that they have evolved their own autistic ideas of truth and rationality, disconnected both from any serious consideration of what education logically implies and from the actual desires of the consumers. That sounds harsh, and of course there are exceptions. But it would be rash to hope for much from this quarter in the immediate future. We must rely on reviving and sophisticating however much common sense and sanity still remains among the general public. It will be the parents and teachers, together with the pupils for whose benefit the whole enterprise is undertaken, who are most likely to change things for the better.

Part C
Practical Methods

In this part of the book we want to outline two practical methods that might help teachers to improve the thought and feeling of their pupils (perhaps of themselves also) in relation to authority. Many teachers will be more experienced than us, and anyway only particular teachers know their own particular pupils, so that it is difficult to describe these methods without sounding over-general or, in one way or another, irrelevant to the teaching style of some teachers. Each teacher has his or her own style and can only work within it. Nevertheless, we have tried to choose methods that are of sufficiently general application for them to be useful, even if they have to be adapted to the needs of particular teachers and pupils. It is really the *basic ideas* behind or incorporated in the methods that we want to clarify. Any competent teacher will be able to adjust and explicate them as best suits the case.

CHAPTER 8
The Use of Literature

The value of literature for our purposes is, centrally, that it enables us to develop a certain type of understanding and awareness that is part of our awareness of our own and others' feelings. This means that pupils must learn to do more than appreciate such literary elements as a neat plot, a well-turned phrase, a dramatic scene, an amusing portrait; more, also, than just *be moved* by the play or poem or novel. Events in everyday life move us. The merit of literature is that it moves us in a way that may contribute to our understanding. Pupils – and teachers too – have to understand something of *why* they are moved; to understand *what sort of* emotions and beliefs are at work in the characters. This understanding can only go hand-in-hand with an understanding of these emotions and beliefs in themselves: a person cannot, in this sense, understand what it is to be in love if he or she has experienced nothing even remotely similar in his or her own life. Much of the teaching of literature, in this context, will therefore necessarily consist of helping pupils to parallel the emotions of the characters (their motives, underlying beliefs, etc.) with the emotions of the pupils themselves: helping them to see that what X feels in the story is the same as, or like, what they themselves feel, or what they have felt in the past.

With this in mind, it is possible to bring out the insights in certain pieces of literature in a way that will help the pupils' emotional understanding. We need to use texts that are popular with the pupils, as well as valuable for our own purposes; and we should not be frightened of using what some may feel is 'bad' literature. The important thing is to use whatever will make the pupils' emotions more visible to them. Fortunately there are at least some books that are both 'good' literature and good teaching material. Here is an example of some notes on Golding's *Lord of the Flies*, which teachers may find useful.

Lord of the Flies, *by William Golding*

Golding's novel is deservedly popular for use with pupils, because it is directly and straightforwardly relevant to their own situation. It is about boys of school age, about their relationships with each other and the (absent) adult world, about their behaviour in reality and in fantasy. Hence it is not easy for pupils to 'miss the point': the events and characters in the island-world speak for themselves.

It would be a waste of time to repeat the more obvious 'points' that Golding brings out so skilfully. Inevitably one would merely repeat, in a duller and less compelling form, things that are better said in the novel itself. What the teacher may usefully do, however, is to try to *generalize* these and less obvious points under a number of headings that will be useful for the pupils' moral life in general. For although pupils may need little encouragement to respond to the novel, they will need to be shown the applicability of it to life as a whole. It is dangerously easy not only to respond to the island-world but also to *remain in it*.

RULES

In this island-world or society there is an attempt to make and keep various rules and contracts: to keep the fire going, to give the right to speak only to the boy who holds the conch, to obey the elected chief (Ralph), and so on. This progressively breaks down, until at the end Piggy and the conch (both representing 'law and order') are destroyed. Of course there are various underlying psychological causes for this, but it is worth considering the making and breaking of rules in their own right.

Piggy sees at once the need for planning and action. 'We got to find the others. We got to do something. . . . Have a meeting.' He is purposeful. He wants rules because rules are necessary to get things done. Ralph sees something of the point of this, but is occasionally in a dream world ('Daddy . . . he's a commander in the Navy. When he gets leave he'll come and rescue us.'). Jack, although he is open to such possibilities as friendship and co-operation with Ralph, has no real concept of rules and contracts at all: as head choir-boy, he sees the only purpose of rules as an excuse to enforce his will ('We'll have rules', he cried excitedly. 'Lots of rules! Then when anyone breaks 'em; Whee-oh! Wacco! Bong! Doink!'). It is not really clear to anyone except Piggy that *rules are for fulfilling certain purposes*, and this is why they break down so quickly. The purposes get forgotten. Ralph forgets the *point* of having a fire; Jack says, 'We've got to have rules and obey them. After all, we're not savages. We're English; and the English are best at everything. So we've got to do the right things.'

These boys have been used to obeying rules imposed by adults, but have had no practice in making and obeying their own rules, and consequently have no understanding of rules. We might say they have no *political* understanding, for the whole basis of politics, whether in large states or small island-worlds, depends on some contractual basis. This in turn depends on the ability and the desire to *communicate* and *reflect* sufficiently. When the boys first meet, Ralph tells them that they must make a fire. 'At once half the boys were on their feet. Jack clamoured among them, the conch forgotten. "Come on! Follow me!" ' They cannot wait to talk and think: they have to *do* something. 'Like kids', Piggy says scornfully. 'Acting like a crowd of kids!' But Ralph follows them up the mountain. Nor do they have any idea of what sort of leader it would be wise to appoint. 'I ought to be chief', said Jack with simple arrogance, 'because I'm chapter chorister and head boy. I can sing C sharp.' And they accept Ralph because he is reassuring, large, attractive and possesses the semi-magical conch.

The breakdown of rules is, above everything, the breakdown of decision procedures. The *constitution* is violated. The elected chief is not obeyed, the assemblies are not held, there are no proper rules of procedure. It is a matter not so much of agreeing to do the wrong thing – making the wrong sort of contract – as of failing to make any serious and lasting agreement at all. (If Jack had been unchallenged chief from the first, the resulting society might have been in many respects evil, but it might also have been more coherent.) Part of the reason for the incoherence is the failure to back the rules by proper sanctions. Ralph and Piggy are not realists: Ralph is anxious to placate Jack, and Piggy hopes (even believes, to begin with) that people will be sensible enough to keep the rules. Consequently there are no means of enforcement, no way of checking the impulse-governed actions that wreck the constitution and destroy the society.

The chief lesson here is perhaps the immense *complexity* of any society, small or large. Pupils are used to a tradition of law and order that has been built up slowly and painfully since the earliest times, and that even now is easily broken down. If people were reasonable, if they could reflect and communicate like Piggy, if they could hold steadily in their minds the ends they desired and calmly agree on the means to achieve them, politics would be simple. But people are not like that. Knowing that we are not, we rightly devise various mechanisms to keep ourselves on the right lines – the mechanisms that appear, in complex and large-scale societies, as voting, courts of law, elected representatives, legitimized authority, police and law-enforcement bodies, and debate. All these, if only in simple forms, are required for any social group, however small. Practice by acting or role-playing, or (better) by taking some responsibility in real life or in 'simulation situations' for social order and control, may bring these points home to pupils and help them to bridge the gap between the primitive insights gained from the novel and their real-life behaviour.

THE UNCONSCIOUS

This is a convenient title for that part of the human mind from which our less reasonable fears and desires flow, fears and desires that constantly upset the attitudes and beliefs that we consciously entertain and approve. Golding makes it clear that the power of the unconscious, in the island-world, is too great for rules and contracts to have any success; and he takes pains to bring out the extent, force and variety of its unreason.

These forces are so powerful in the minds of all the dwellers in the island-world that the 'good', or at least 'natural', desires rapidly become insubstantial and too weak to cope. The early exploration of the island by Ralph and Jack, which has something of the boy-hood delight and joy of Ballantyne's *Coral Island* (of which *Lord of the Flies* is in some sense a modern version), seems to us right and proper. The talk of 'my dad' and 'my auntie', and even Jack's rather out-of-place references to his choir, mean for us that they still retain some grasp of the adult world, that they are still striving to be 'good', to be secure. Even the pig-hunting, at least to begin with, seems like a sensible economic measure, like something out of *The Swiss Family Robinson*. But the boys have no defence against the unconscious. Maurice says, 'I don't believe in the beast of course. As Piggy says, life's scientific, but we don't know, do we? Not certainly, I mean . . .'. And so the defences are swept away.

From this point of view the novel is pessimistic. Even at the end, when the boys are miraculously reduced to size by the sudden appearance of the British officer, there is no suggestion of how things might have gone better. All that the officer can find to say is, 'I should have thought that a pack of British boys – you're all British aren't you? – would have been able to put up a better show than that – I mean . . .'. His values are no better. 'He turned away to give them time to pull themselves together; and waited, allowing his eyes to rest on the trim cruiser in the distance' – symbol of Britain, law and order, and 'pulling oneself together'. What Golding calls 'man's essential illness' seems incurable.

But it would be wrong for the teacher to take this (or anything else) as the book's moral message. The book, like all literature, *shows us how things are.* It is true, and important, that in respect of 'the darkness of the human heart' things are worse than some of us (perhaps particularly the more 'virtuous' pupils and adults) like to think, and certainly worse than we like to face. But it is also true that we can cope with this darkness, if only slowly, piecemeal, and with great difficulty: we need not (indeed must not) merely deny it and turn our backs on it, pretending that 'there isn't any beast'. We have to face it, study it, feel it, gain insights into it, and thus eventually control it better.

HEROES

Realization of the power of the unconscious may profitably be used to change some of the thoughts and feelings pupils may have in identifying with certain characters, or in regarding them as 'heroes'. There are, of course, obvious senses in which one character or another may be seen as (in some naive way) 'heroic', but a closer inspection of the island-world may alter our values here.

The simplest 'hero' is Jack. He operates on an 'honour' ethic, in which simple-minded concepts like 'being captain', 'killing more pigs', 'hunting', 'not being cowardly', etc., predominate. The inadequacy of this is shown clearly enough. Ralph is a somewhat more sophisticated 'hero', and perhaps the character who most catches our sympathy because he is torn between various conflicting emotions. Near the end he comes out on the 'right side' if only with Piggy's help. ' "Which is better – to have rules and agree, or to hunt and kill?'' . . . Ralph shouted against the noise. ''Which is better, law and rescue, or hunting and breaking things up?'' ' But it is too late: he has let things slide, because he is tainted with Jack's 'honour' ethic: the idea of 'being cowardly' horrifies him too.

Piggy is the more obviously 'right' character, if too weak to count as a 'hero'. It is he who makes all the sensible suggestions, and only he who has any real concern for others. After the fire on the mountain, only Piggy notices that one of the 'littluns' is absent: 'And that's not all. Them kids. The little 'uns. Who took any notice of 'em? Who knows how many we got?'. Moreover, Piggy has a clear concept of morality and some degree of bravery to realize it: 'I'm going to him with this conch in my hands. I'm going to hold it out. Look, I'm goin' to say, you're stronger than I am and you haven't got asthma. You can see, I'm going to say, and with both eyes. But I don't ask for my glasses back, not as a favour. I don't ask you to be a sport, I'll say, not because you're stronger but because what's right's right. Give me my glasses, I'm going to say – you got to!' He is the only one who has a proper understanding of *reason* and *justice*: Ralph has some vague idea of 'being sensible', and the others merely rely on impulse or authority. In a sense Piggy is a moral hero, a martyr to the cause of reason. But he is unrealistic. 'Give me my glasses . . . you got to!' means 'you got to *if* you're going to be reasonable, just, fair, etc.'. But the if is too big an if for Jack and his gang, too big for all the other characters – too big, indeed, for most adults in our own world, at least for most of the time. People do not *want* to be reasonable, just, fair, etc.

The tragedy of Piggy is the tragedy of all thinkers, from Socrates onwards, who have tried to lead people into the ways of justice and enlightenment, sweet reason and good sense. The point is not that these are not desirable objectives, or that there is something wrong or inadequate with the notion of 'being reasonable' (indeed, such a view could not be intelligibly maintained, since the whole business of argument and thinking rests on rationality). Jack cannot – does not want to – answer Piggy's demand of 'which is better . . .?' He cannot enter into rational debate about the comparative merits of one life as against another, for that would be, at once, to concede to good sense and reason, which alone allow such debate. He and his gang just make loud noises and throw spears. They follow their desires, their impulses, their fantasies. They are not even *trying* to think. The tragedy lies not in Piggy's ideals but in his failure to realize the extent of the opposition. It is not, really, that there are other policies, other theories, that impede our progress to sanity. It is rather that the unconscious sweeps anything that could seriously count as a 'policy' or a 'theory' out of the way, and replaces it by fantasy and impulse-governed behaviour. Piggy, like Socrates, was killed. He made his gesture, asked his questions, and received a rock that destroyed him. 'He fell forty feet and landed on his back across that square, red rock in the sea. His head opened and stuff came out and turned red.' *That* is the extent of the opposition to reason. We would apparently rather have *that* than do anything so difficult as think, plan, control, consider.

This leads us to one other candidate for 'heroism', Simon. He has no especial bravery, and no qualities of leadership. He has not the good sense, the skin-deep rationality of Piggy, and he achieves little. But it is he who is the nearest to *understanding* what is happening. 'Simon felt a perilous necessity to speak. . . . "Maybe", he said hesitantly, "maybe there is a beast." The assembly cried out savagely and Ralph stood up in amazement. . . . "What I mean is . . . maybe it's only us." "Nuts!" That was from Piggy, shocked out of decorum. Simon went on, "We could be sort of . . .'. Simon became inarticulate in his effort to express mankind's essential illness. Inspiration came to him. "What's the dirtiest thing there is?" As an answer Jack dropped into the uncomprehending silence that followed it the one crude expressive syllable. Release was like an orgasm. Those littluns who had climbed back on the twister fell off again and did not mind. The hunters were screaming with delight. Simon's effort fell about him in ruins; the laughter beat him cruelly and he shrank away defenceless to his seat.'

If Piggy's attempt to preserve justice meets with failure, so too – and still more quickly – does Simon's attempt to introduce a minimum of insight into their situation. He is trying to say that, inside all of them, there is something nasty, dirty, horrifying, beastly. Jack's use of a schoolboy's 'dirty word' arouses only hysterical laughter, the laughter that still comes from both pupils and adults (either laughter or shocked disapproval) when anything 'dirty', sexual or scatological, is mentioned, and that acts (as on the island) as a defence, preventing the assembly from taking Simon seriously. The attempt to show truth is brutally chopped down. The boys have dissociated themselves too sharply from the 'dirty' side of life - for them it is now something to be disowned by laughter or fear. They cannot even begin to face it.

So Simon goes on to discover the truth alone. He faces the horrors - the temporary insanity, almost - of a confrontation with the imaginary Lord of the Flies, loses consciousness, but grimly plods on. He sees the dead parachutist and faces the facts - horrible enough, but not as horrible as the imagined beast. 'He turned to the poor broken thing that sat stinking by his side. The beast was harmless and horrible; and the news must reach the others as soon as possible. He started down the mountain'. But when he arrives they are already in a manic and hysteric state: 'Kill the beast! Cut his throat! Spill his blood! Do him in.' So they kill him. 'There were no words, and no movements but the tearing of teeth and claws.'

Ralph had a fair chance, Piggy a faint chance, Simon hardly a chance at all. Those we resist most, those we try to destroy most avidly, are those who would make us face the truth about ourselves. It hurts to face such truth. Indeed - an insight at least as old as Aeschylus's 'we learn by suffering' - the pain is to some degree a criterion of how much truth we can accept. This sort of heroism, which is a necessary prerequisite for any serious moral progress, is perhaps the most important concept that can emerge from the novel. If the pupils can gain a firm grasp of it, with the teacher's help, they will have gained something of very great and permanent value.

What happens when a teacher tries to use this method in class? Here is an account by one teacher of how he used these notes on *Lord of the Flies*.

Lord of the Flies with boys of 14 and 15

PUPILS AND BACKGROUND

These were boys of 14 and 15 in a low form (Vc) at a middle-grade private boarding school. There were 35 in the form. The average IQ was 103, but scoring on 'verbal' items in the IQ tests was significantly lower than scoring on other items (shapes, mazes, etc.): I should regard these pupils as of average or below average 'literary intelligence'. They studied mostly scientific subjects.

The social class of these pupils is hard to describe exactly: perhaps generally lower-middle or middle-middle. Few or none of their parents had received any 'elitist' education (at a private school or grammar school). The parents had made some money (having themselves risen from more humble origins), usually in small-scale business. Home background was not 'cultural'.

More importantly, however, there were – on the surface, at least – comparatively few problems of authority or discipline. The pupils were not anti-school or anti-establishment. This was, I believe, in great measure owing not so much to the child-rearing of the parents as to the firm and effective enforcement by the school of its own authority, on both pupils and parents. At this school one simply did not cause (much) trouble; amongst other things, the headteacher would have descended like the wrath of God. Teachers were well-known, and on the whole respected; gross disobedience was not viable for long. This did not, of course, prevent individuals and whole classes from making life hell for particular teachers, but it provided an important background of tacit acceptance.

This somewhat unfashionable but in my view crucially important acceptance of authority enabled me – with the help of whatever personality features in myself may have contributed (some hindered) – to do a great deal more with this average or below-average class than I have found possible in some other schools. I was able to *get more done more quickly*, without the constant need to cajole, threaten, wheedle, resign or bore. Because, and only because, the authority was ultimately taken for granted, I could drop any authoritarian image, forget about 'demanding respect', be human, use any language I liked (I swear quite a lot when I get excited) and generally let my hair down. More importantly, I could 'bounce' individual pupils or the whole class into doing lots of different things without a lot of fuss and tiresome objections. I could say, for instance, 'OK, you two, Bloggs and Figgins, take your coats off, start fighting – oh, for God's sake, *fighting*, not caressing, if you're in love with each other you can go to your housemaster about it, now start throwing punches', and so on.

I stress this general point not because it is fun for the teacher to be able to let his hair down, but because the respect for authority is necessary in order to form a warm, coherent human group that can actually *do* and *learn* things, and without such a group any teaching of any book is likely to become remote, cold, semi-paralysed, impossibly 'abstract'. But the authority must be firmly there in the first place, even if – particularly if – we are to explore anti-authority feelings via *Lord of the Flies*, *Unman, Wittering & Zigo* or any suitable text. Firm authority followed by (associated with) warmth and humanity seem necessary prerequisites for any serious learning of this kind.

GENERAL DESCRIPTION

The authority was initially useful in getting the pupils to read the text properly. I had two weeks (10 periods) in which to deal with it in class. I told them to read it thoroughly before then. One or two hadn't. ('Well, Figgins, you say you've read it, what do you think about the character of Archibald? Is he nice or nasty?' 'Nasty, I think, sir.' 'But what about his relationship with Alice? Doesn't that show him in a better light?' 'H'm, well, sir, yes, perhaps.' 'Figgins, there aren't any Archibald and Alice in the thing at all. Are you going to sit here for two weeks while we talk about a book you haven't even read? Get it properly read by the time we start otherwise I'll half-kill you.' So he did.

Getting the text read was easy anyway, because the book appealed to them very quickly. Some had doubts: 'It's just a school story, isn't it, like the *Coral Island*', said one boy with unconscious intelligence, his father's Scotts and Ballantynes and Hentys collecting dust on his shelves at home. But by the time we started work most of them had read and enjoyed it, although none of them was a quick reader. (Their standard reading consisted of comics, football magazines, pin-up magazines and a few thrillers.)

We started in a very pedestrian way by dealing with any bits they hadn't understood (words they didn't know, sentences they couldn't construe, obscurities in the plot). Here again I could rely on a tradition that they would *say* if they didn't understand something. They knew that if they asked they'd get a proper and non-angry answer, and get credit for asking, whereas if they didn't ask and were found not to have understood, blood would flow. Sometimes there were bits of the plot, or characters, that I had forgotten about, and I'd ask them to amend my own ignorance: they jumped at this chance of patronage ('It's really very simple sir, it's actually a dead man from an aeroplane . . .'). After this we all had a fairly firm grip on what the book overtly said.

Then we tried the first 'bounce'. 'OK, now all you virtuous chaps know what the book says, so we'll start trying to *feel* something, OK? You don't have to be alarmed, Figgins, you do *have* feelings, you know, you haven't lost them like you lose your textbooks. We'll start with the schools we were at a few years ago – well, more than a few for me. Let me see, what *was* it like when I was 12? Oh, yes, it was pretty good hell, I was a sort of Piggy, I think, a white-faced intellectual . . .' (short account by me of this). 'What about you, Bloggs?' 'Well, sir, it was all right, I suppose.' 'Figgins?' 'Oo no, sir, it was terrible, the big boys used to lock up the little ones and . . .' (long horror story by Figgins). 'When you two write your autobiographies they'll look jolly different. Mr Bloggs, asked about the details of his school days, said that they were all right he supposed. Mr Figgins, on the other hand, said that the incidence of torture and sexual vice among the middle classes. . . . It is actually quite hard to remember, isn't it? Sometimes one invents; sometimes one doesn't really want to remember. Let's try some more.' After a while most boys are able to reproduce some of the feelings they had, or thought they had, when they were 12 or 13. A few scenes directly relevant to the text emerged: bullying, school-chants, rule-breaking.

Next time a harder 'bounce'. 'OK, we'll take bullying. Who gets bullied here, and who are bullies?' Silence: this is too quick for them. 'Well, all forms I've ever taught have this going on, it's not something peculiar. I could probably make some good guesses. I mean, sometimes when I'm just coming in the class I hear the odd squeal and giggle and so on. This is something lots of people do. Take Mr Snooks on the staff, for instance. I've often noticed that the staff aren't nice to him in the common room. Perhaps' (my eye roams round the class) – 'no, I don't want to guess, you tell me.' Bloggs: 'Well, sir, I suppose I'm not always very nice to East here' (this is putting it mildly). 'What do you feel, East?' 'Oh, sir, no, it's all right.' (Long pause.) 'Nobody's very comfortable about this, are they? It's not just that Bloggs or anyone feels guilty about bullying. Isn't it that you don't like looking at the thing at all? You want to keep the emotions under cover.' (Vague mutterings.)

'OK, let's get at them this way. I'll start by bullying

Figgins – actually I suppose I do a bit of this anyway, don't I?' (One or two gratified smiles of recognition.) I approach Figgins, *à la* Mr Bumble: 'Now, boy . . .': there follows a short scene in which I act some sadism towards Figgins. 'You weren't quite sure how much of that was real, were you, Figgins? (grin from Figgins). It's OK, actually, it's all under control, we're not actually on Golding's island, you know. Right, now, you try it. I'll leave you to fix up a bullying scene – make it like the ones you actually have, with the same people if you can stand the idea. I'll give you three minutes to prepare.' They do with East and another boy.

'That was very convincing, now let's talk about it. Was it like the scene in Golding where they can't catch a pig so they use one of the boys instead? Let's look at that.' (We look at it and discuss it.) 'Yes, it is nice when they squirm, isn't it? What about the victim? Is it just horrid, East, or is there a sort of peculiar excitement about it? Try and be honest.' East mutters, 'You sometimes feel it's sort of nice being done things to: I don't want it, though', he adds aggressively, looking at Bloggs. 'Well, a bit of you does, and most of you doesn't, isn't that it? And you Bloggs, the same, isn't it? You don't *say* "I have now decided, after due consideration, to bully East." You just find yourself doing it, it's a sort of drug.'

This leads on to (in adult terminology) a discussion of the unconscious, tied in with a consideration of the novel and the points about the unconscious in the notes. They slowly get the hang of the idea that there are 'horrid' things inside one that one doesn't like to face (the Beast). They go some way towards being able to own up about what these 'horrid' things, as represented in their fantasies, actually are. To some degree they are still inhibited at a superficial level (apt to giggle about sex, etc.) so I have to start the ball rolling here by confessing to or inventing fantasies of my own, where these are relevant to the novel and the notes.

After a few periods I can say, 'Perhaps now we can face each other without too much fear or giggling, so let's put the chairs in a circle (this is very unusual in this school) where we can see each other.' We do this and talk for a while about how we feel under this arrangement. Among other illuminating remarks, Flashman says, 'It's awful, we're all frightened of each other: we either want to get closer or much further away.' 'But you mix with each other every day all the time.' 'Yes, but this is different: you don't know what you feel, somehow.' They can only stand just so much of this (significantly they begin to drop the 'sir' in this situation): at short intervals I have to dismantle it by talking more directly about the novel, reading bits aloud, or returning them to their desks to write notes so that they can escape.

For the first week I have to spend quite a bit of time 'bouncing': I get them to act, prepared or impromptu; to play roles (characters in the novel or others); to wrestle, engage in slanging matches, and so on; to chant 'Kill the pig! Cut his throat! Bash him in!', interspersed with fairly strong leads ('How would it be if we chanted "Bash *her* in!"?'). We do quite a bit on rules: what rules do they follow when they are by themselves, e.g. in between class periods, in their studies, etc.? How far do they take the rules in the school for granted, rebel against them and so on? (We take care here to prevent the discussion becoming 'academic', i.e. a lot of general long-range talk about ideal rules for a school and so on; we steer it back to the particular case, the particular emotions aroused by rules as a whole and particular rules. 'How did you feel when the headmaster told you off?', 'Did you like enforcing rules when you were senior boys in your last schools?')

For the second week I was able to be much more 'non-directive', almost entirely because the pupils would speak more freely and relevantly. Some at least of the more superficial defences had been dropped: they became able to admit to fantasies in some detail. Many of these turn out to be common, which is a relief to them. They find some reassurance in knowing (not just in the abstract, but by hearing the details) that other people too have torture-fantasies, or feel frightened that something inside them will explode, or whatever it may be. They begin to get some understanding of standard psychological patterns or 'moves', like projection. The point about the Beast being *inside* them, although they may project it on to others outside, becomes more real to them. They gain some notion of the concept of ambivalence, the possibility of hating and loving the same object or person.

Here the dangers and defences are different. Some pupils are tempted to invent, to show off their 'confessional' abilities (as in revivalist meetings), to try to shock. They get angry if I do not react. Many get the idea that it is only the 'bad' things we have to own up to: they will admit that they get fed up with me as a teacher, feel murderous when I bully them, etc., but find it harder to admit to more sentimental feelings. They are as afraid of loving as they are of being 'bad', or more so. We investigate in more detail the passages in the book that deal with the comradeship on the island, the sensual pleasures. Golding's boys do not express much affection either.

I have made this part of the work sound far too generalized. In practice, we returned constantly to particular passages in the novel, tying these up with particular scenes in school life. ('Don't you treat some masters the way they treated Piggy without his spectacles? In what light do you see Mr Snooks, now that we have discussed this?') We act these scenes out, and there is a gradual improvement in the pupils' ability to *comment on* what they feel. The transference becomes obvious, not by being lectured about as 'the transference', but when a pupil says, for instance, 'Is that the sort of thing you wanted me to say?' or 'Why should I tell you how I feel, when you don't always tell us how you feel?' (angrily), or 'It's jolly nice to have you here, sir, we can really get close this way, can't we?' (said with more embarrassed feeling than the 'public school' style suggests).

In this case I found that the transference was worth overt consideration, but I made a bad mistake in supposing that much could be done to connect the pupils' feelings with their childhood. They might occasionally refer to their parents – particularly when discussing rules – but they were unable or unwilling to make any emotional connections. My mistake was to plug away at this too hard. Boys whose relationships with their fathers (as I happened to know) mirrored exactly their relationships with authority generally must surely, I thought, be able to feel (not just to see in principle) this connection. I tried to 'bounce' this, but usually met a brick wall. Thus, in discussing the very end of the book, where the arrival of the adult shrinks the boys back to size, discussion led to adults in authority and then to parents. I might then say, 'Come on Figgins, tell us what you feel about your father and mother.' 'Oh, they're all right, sir.' 'Do you love them?' 'Oh, yes, sir.' I was (just) sensible enough not to make the pupils feel guilty or incompetent if they did not talk about their feelings here, but I wasted a lot of their time in trying to probe defences that – for these pupils at least – were not ready to come down.

Another mistake I made was of the opposite kind. In discussion of the Ralph–Piggy and Ralph–Jack relationships, and of various other scenes in the novel, the pupils said much (in an indirect way) that at least bordered upon close physical relationships ('sexuality' is too narrow a word). I am conscious of quasi-deliberately steering them away from this, although such steering crippled and impoverished much they said or wanted to say about feelings of love and affection. The shyness between Ralph and Jack, the physical attractiveness of Ralph that helps to make him the leader, the feel of the squirming flesh when the pig-substitute is caught – all this was certainly in their minds, and needed to be brought out.

Both these mistakes were due to more than mere insensitivity on my part. On reflection, I can see desires and fears that prevented me from taking the right course. Some of these are obvious: a doctrinaire desire to encourage 'talk about childhood', probably more relevant to a proper psychotherapeutic context than to this; a (natural) fear that overt discussion of 'homosexual' feelings would be frowned on by parents and school authorities, and cause trouble generally. But the major causes were less conscious feelings of my own about childhood, homosexuality and other relevant issues. I will not bore the reader with these in detail, but the general point is immensely important for all such teaching.

In the above I have emphasized only the time spent (short enough, goodness knows) on the use of the text as a springboard for moral awareness. How much time each teacher will want to spend on this, as against considering the text from other points of view, will depend on circumstances and the teacher's interests. With an essentially similar class of boys I was able to spend nearly twice as long on the book. In both cases it was being set for an examination, but in the second case I spent more time on more strictly 'literary' considerations, making them write notes and essays and so forth. It did not seem to me to be true that the 'moral awareness' time suffered from being spread out over four weeks rather than two. As long as we discussed (acted, etc.) feelings two or three times a week, all was well – they did not seem to 'forget' them in the intervening periods. When feelings were discussed only once a week or less, however, I thought I detected enough 'forgetfulness' to show this up as a bad policy.

Equally, it is possible to overdo such discussion. Trying to do this at full pressure for five days in a row (nearly an hour a day) produced, with this teacher and these pupils, counter-productive results; the pupils became slightly hysterical, over-quick, reacting shallowly and superficially. It was exciting but not, I think, as educationally valuable as a slower tempo. If I had to guess at an ideal arrangement, I would say something like two or three times a week. But this is a guess hardly worth making: we need further research.

Besides the techniques described, of acting, role-play, chairs-in-a-circle, etc., I found tape-recordings useful: greater objectivity was possible, and more insight, when the pupils could hear their own reactions later. We had several productive sessions commenting on our own previous discussion. I did not find discussion in any way inhibited by recording, except perhaps for the first few minutes of the first recorded session.

Rightly or wrongly, I felt that the discussed feelings should be restricted ('officially', as it were) to the classroom, and discouraged attempts by pupils to raise them with me 'after hours'.

Finally, I must apologize for quoting examples of my somewhat breezy and facetious teaching style. Many readers may dislike it (I do myself at times), but I cannot think how else to get the 'feel' of the periods across. I do not think that much turns on this style or that, except perhaps that styles show something significant about the personality of the teacher. But that goes deeper than we need burrow here.

CONCLUSIONS

I am not sure whether there are any 'conclusions' here that are not mere repetition, but the following points might be worth highlighting.

- A firm background of respect for authority was needed to start with. (I would guess that, where this is insufficiently present, the teacher would do better to try to solve the authority problem with the pupils before trying to engage on any specific teaching forms whatever; otherwise he or she will be trying to build on what does not exist.)

- It is desirable that the text be read and (overtly) understood before we use it for the purposes of moral education.

- The natural declension seemed to be: (1) text, (2) acting or role-playing scenes in the text, (3) acting or role-playing parallel scenes from the pupils' real-life experience, (4) comments by pupils on their (and others') feelings in this acting/role-play, and (5) discussion of feelings not tied to particular scenes. This declension was the easiest (least inhibiting, 'new' or frightening) for these pupils at least, and I suspect generally. This does not mean, of course, that one should not mix up the order. Naturally one moves back and forth from one to another, as occasion demands. But the general direction or movement is from the text to their 'real-life' feelings and back again.

- As long as the teacher keeps the rule about not *pressurizing* pupils to talk about their feelings, and as long as he or she does not comment moralistically on what they say, I reckon the dangers to be minimal. But much depends on being able to establish some 'warm' context of communication in the first place, in which not only the authority but also the 'togetherness' is taken for granted.

- The teacher (if he or she is like me, anyway) has to resist the temptation to over-interpret: that is, to *tidy up* too much what the pupils say, thereby removing it from their own insight and giving it the teacher's own set of labels. In particular, concepts ('ambivalence', etc.) should only be introduced – if at all – when it is quite clear that the class knows what the concept is (but hasn't got a word for it).

- The teacher must beware of steering against the natural current of talk (my two major errors). There are no rules for this: the teacher has to rely on his or her own insight and knowledge of his or her own types of unreason.

- It is useful (often essential) for the teacher to *give a lead* in talking about his or her own feelings, as an equal.

- It is essential for teachers to remain in control of themselves at all times, so that they may be a source of security for the pupils. They can be excited or enthusiastic or funny, or all sorts of things, but they must feel secure.

CHAPTER 9
Rules and Contracts in Practice

Here we shall be concerned with a more *direct* attempt to teach our pupils about authority. We know that there are two kinds of 'authority' about which we should have no worries. First is the 'authority' that a person has in a group, resulting from agreement or acceptance by the group of certain delegated and legitimized powers. An elected leader or the accepted captain of a games team are examples. Second is the 'authority' that a person has by virtue of superior knowledge in a particular area: thus A may be an authority on Polish history, B an authority on vintage cars, etc. In both these cases there are good reasons why the authorities should be listened to and obeyed, to the extent that is covered by their authority. And it is important for children to learn this, to learn that they cannot consistently accept and legitimize an authority, and then not obey it, and that some people know more about certain things than they do, and that (given this) it is unreasonable not to accept what they say.

What is essential is to distinguish these from another thing that might perhaps be called 'authority' and is certainly in people's minds when they talk about 'authority': the deployment of naked power, prestige, charisma or 'moral pressure', when this is *not* legitimized as above. An 'authority' (better, someone who *pretends* to be an authority) in this sense attempts to gain obedience when there is no rationale for obedience. He or she says 'do it because I say so' or 'because I'm your parent' when these are not reasons for obeying. Similarly an elected team captain has genuine authority, but the big bully in the team may influence others by toughness and personality – but this is better termed 'influence', 'power' or, at the most, '*de facto* authority' (if the team in fact obeys the bully rather than the elected captain).

If a child is to learn to accept legitimate authority, and to resist 'influence' wherever possible, he has somehow to learn the *conceptual* distinctions between them: to learn to *identify* particular cases of them. We have to educate the child out of thinking solely in terms of obeying or not obeying, conforming or rebelling, and encourage him or her to distinguish between different *types* of obedience backed by different *reasons*. It is not, of course, likely that we can do this in as brief and direct a way as we have suggested above – that is, simply by pointing them out orally or on paper. We have, therefore, to instantiate these distinctions in different games, different social contexts, in order that the child may see them in action.

We need therefore not only contexts or games that show only *one* of the forms of authority in operation, but also contexts or games that show how one of them may get confused with another, with regrettable consequences. For example, suppose we play a game in which the group are given a certain task – say, to decorate and furnish their classroom. Assume that this task is voluntarily accepted by all the group, and that they are given some money to help carry it out. Now the group will need certain of its members in positions of authority. If they think the context warrants it, they may choose a plenipotentiary leader, or they may form a committee, or they may discuss everything as equals and operate by common consent, merely appointing people to be in charge of specific tasks, such as accounting for the money they have been given. But to a greater or lesser extent, there will be contracted and legitimized authorities. Secondly, one person will have had more experience of furniture buying, or painting, or how to hang pictures. They will discover this and accept his or her authority in these areas. But also, unless the group is too strictly controlled, there will be certain members of the group who exercise a strong influence. This influence may work with the 'legitimate authorities' if, for instance, a member uses his or her strong personality and enthusiasm to further the task of the group; or it may work against them, if he or she 'sets a bad example'.

All this is in essence very simple and (in a sense) common knowledge to every teacher and indeed every pupil. What is important is that all of it should be make *explicit*. The importance of this game is not that the classroom gets decorated. It is that members of the group, the players, are enabled to become aware of what is happening in respect of the three forms of authority, of how the concept of 'authority' is being attended to or disregarded during the task. To make it explicit, we can think of various methods: stopping the group directly after something has happened relevant to authority and commenting on it, discussing what has happened after the whole task is completed, advising at particular points before trouble arises, taking a tape-recording or a video-recording of the group during its performance and playing it back with discussion afterwards, appointing an 'outside' member of the group to write its 'history' in relation to authority, and so on. We shall not comment on the merits or demerits of these and other techniques here. The purpose of the exercise should be plain enough.

If the points and logic that lie behind this kind of teaching are sufficiently clear, we shall not need to spend very much time on detailed descriptions of methods. In what follows we aim to do not much more than remind the teacher of certain practical moves that will necessarily follow from what we have noticed above.

Rules and contracts within the institution

The authorities responsible for the rules of the institution will first ensure that these rules have a rational basis. This means, as we have seen, that they must not be first-order 'moralistic' rules, but must be justified by the function of the institution. In the case of each rule, the headteacher (or local education authority, vice-chancellor, principal, or whoever) must ask, 'is this rule required for the efficient functioning of this institution?'

The answer to this will not be directly given by reference to the will or the likes and dislikes of the headteacher, or the pupils' parents, or the pupils, or the staff, or the governors, or the local authorities, or anything of that kind. It will be given by consideration of two classes of factors. First, what is required by (so to speak) 'pure reason', if there is no outside interference? What rules are in fact necessary for staff and pupils, if they are to teach and learn as effectively as possible? Secondly, what is required by public relations or (in a wide sense of the term) 'politics' – that is, what is forced on the institution by the views of others and their power, however irrational?

An absolutely clear-cut distinction must be made, both in theory and practice, between these two. For instance, one might believe that certain rules about dress and manners were not required by 'pure reason', that learning would go on in the institution as efficiently, perhaps more efficiently, if the pupils were allowed to do what they liked in this area. But one might, under certain circumstances, also believe that these rules *were* required by 'politics', that parents, the town council or some other body insisted on certain standards of dress and manners, and would do the institution severe damage if these standards were not met.

Of course the person in authority has to weigh up such cases, balancing factors in one against factors in the other. There is no determinate solution to all problems. What is important is that these quite different types of reason should be distinguished in the person's mind, *and presented to the pupils for what they are*. Thus if the only reason for having a particular rule is that the parents insist on it, and that this insistence must be met (otherwise perhaps they will withdraw their children or not contribute to a new swimming-pool), then the authority must *say just this* to the pupils. Without this kind of honesty it will be very hard for the pupils to grasp the rationality of rules at all (and hard also for them to resist the impression that many adults are hypocritical).

It is far from enough to make sure that the rules are rational, and present them to the pupils as such. The authorities must also: make sure that they carry specified sanctions with them, so that everybody can know exactly what the penalty is for breaking this or that rule; make sure that the sanctions are actually enforced (preferably with a minimum of argument); make sure that these rules and sanctions are, both individually and collectively, absolutely clearly specified, and understood by every pupil. If this is done it will save endless time and trouble and, above all, it will give practical shape to the crucial distinction between having an established contract and set of rules that everybody agrees (however unwillingly) to keep, so that law and order is maintained and the institution can get on with the job, and contexts in which argument about the rules is allowed and encouraged, pupils are taught to criticize rules, make up their own rules, and so forth. It is the blurring of this distinction that leads to the time-wasting, and sometimes the near-chaos, that is a feature of many contemporary institutions.

A vital point here, which we noticed earlier, is the inclusion of second-order rules; that is, rules-about-changing-rules. These, like the first-order rules, must meet the criteria we have listed – they must be rationally based, rationally presented, and include specified and enforced sanctions. Thus the scope granted to different bodies (the school council, the student union, etc.) or to different methods (protests, demonstrations, strikes) in changing the rules must be clearly defined, and specific instances marked as legitimate or illegitimate. While it is not possible here, any more than with the first-order rules, to specify *every* case in advance, it is both possible and desirable to specify as many as possible. Thus we may not want to say in advance whether a 'protest march' is acceptable or not, but we can at least specify anything that involves violence, disruption of normal work or interference with other citizens as illegitimate; as against (say) peaceful meetings in a park, against which we need make no special rules.

Provided all these distinctions are clearly observed, we do not think the authorities should have very much difficulty in determining the actual content of their rules. Thus we may feel reasonably certain that some things are absolutely necessary for almost any educational institution: there must be regular attendance, punctuality, absence of violence or other forms of disruption, and pupils must be in a fit state to do the work. This cuts out truancy, strikes, drunkenness, certain kinds of drug addiction, certain types of demonstration and disobedience. Equally, it would be hard to show that behaviour in the areas of sex, dress, hair style, cosmetics, etc. were relevant to the institution. Of course it is always possible to dispute particular cases: some might say that school uniforms make the institution's work easier (keep the pupils' minds off the current fashions, avoid competition and jealousy between the rich and well-dressed and the poor), while others might maintain the opposite (putting teenagers into uniform is repressive, makes them resent school, etc.). In such cases we may have to guess, or find out more facts. But provided the criteria are clear – provided we do not operate with some vague prejudicial notion of 'what is respectable' or 'what is permitted nowadays' – we do not think that reasonable people would disagree over many important cases.

The set of rules, or contract, that these criteria will generate apply, of course, only *for* the institution and only *within* the institution. The institution is part of a wider society that has its own rules and sanctions. These will probably be hopelessly muddled, partly because our law-makers are not very bright, but the institution cannot help that. It can only try to educate the pupils in respect of the wider society, while clarifying and enforcing its own rules in a more coherent manner. It is the pupil's behaviour as a member of the institution, not as a citizen, with which we are here concerned. As with other institutions (clubs, societies), the pupils thus have (at least) two sets of rules to obey: the general rules of citizenship, and the specific contract which they enter into as members of the particular institution. All this has to be made plain to the pupils.

Not all institutions, of course, set out to *educate*. Those that set out only to train for a particular purpose (e.g. a secretarial college) may, like other non-educational institutions, have no particular interest in framing those rules and contracts that are necessary for education in general, or for moral education in particular. But for educational institutions that are concerned (as we think most should be) with moral education, the rules and contracts are likely to be significantly different. Thus we may well think it important that pupils should be initiated into certain kinds of *tradition*, involving behaviour not strictly required by the necessities of academic work. Here again, the elements of such traditions should not be a matter of our own likes and dislikes, but should be judged by whether they contribute to the ends of moral education. Compulsory chapel services, residence in a hall, organized games or morning assembly *may* contribute to those ends, or they may not. We have to decide for ourselves, but we must decide on this criterion.

Acceptance of the contract

If the authorities of the institution have succeeded in carrying out the above simple suggestions, they will be able to present the pupils with a clear and detailed contract or set of contractual rules, each backed by a solid argument of the appropriate type. This in itself would be a big step forward. But it is not enough. The authorities must secure *acceptance* of the contract.

Acceptance here – and this must be made plain to the pupils – does *not* mean absolute agreement; that is, the pupil does not have to think that all the rules are right, or even that many of them are. To accept the contract means to have, and declare, the sincere intention of keeping the rules, whatever one's opinion may be about their merits. This in turn involves agreement that sanctions should be applied if one does break a rule, and the intention of making restitution as far as possible. If these were not involved, we could not say that a person had sincerely accepted the contract.

What the authorities should say to the pupils, then, is something like this: 'You are going to be a member of this institution. Here are the rules, about which we've thought a great deal, and which we think we can justify to the satisfaction of most reasonable people' (and at some point the rules and justifications would be gone through in detail). 'Now, you may still think that some of them are silly. We shall give you plenty of opportunity to say so, and say why you think so, and there are various mechanisms for changing the rules, in which you can take part' (these also are gone through in detail). 'Of course we don't anticipate that you'll keep all the rules all the time. We are all of us swayed by emotion, selfish, forgetful, etc. But granted all this, do you accept the rules and contract? Do you promise to abide by them? Will you consider yourself bound by them? Or is your attitude rather that you feel justified in breaking some of them if you can get away with it?'

Of course this sounds naive, but it will at least give some impression of what the authorities have to get across. Some general methods of getting the concept of rules across are considered later. Here we would simply advise that the authorities should: present this contract *before* the pupils become members of the institution; continue to present it at regular intervals; have some kind of formal ceremony at which the pupils indicate their acceptance, and actually inscribe their signature on the contract; use the signed contracts when any rule is subsequently broken·by the pupil, to remind him or her in concrete form of what the agreement was. No doubt other methods will suggest themselves to the teacher.

There is naturally a difference, in degree if not in kind, between those institutions at which attendance is compulsory (schools) and those at which it is not (universities). In the latter case, we can say to the students words to the effect of, 'Look, you don't *have* to come here, so if you want to come we must be quite sure that you agree to our rules.' In the former we cannot say this. If someone below the school-leaving age says to us, 'This is very unfair, I'm compelled to agree, because I'm compelled to be a member of this institution', what can we reply? We should say something like, 'Yes, you are compelled, but this is inevitable. In this society, where you happen to have had the good or bad luck to be born, you cannot survive below a certain age unless you are at school. Whether this is the right way to run a society may be disputed. But we think it is right, and if you think it is wrong you must persuade enough people to change it in due course. Meanwhile, we are not just compelling you for our own amusement. We teach you, feed you, look after your health, and so on. Given all this, and things as they actually are, do you not think it reasonable to agree to the contract?'

The pupil may still say – or think – that he or she is not going to agree. We then have to say, 'Very well, I see that you still think it unfair. But now you have a choice. You have to keep the rules to some extent anyway, because you are outnumbered, and force is on our side. Do you want to keep them voluntarily, even if you think it in principle unfair; or would you rather be in a permanent state of war with us? We do not ask you to agree with all the rules, or even any of them. Nor do we ask you to think that you are getting a fair deal. All we ask is that you form the intention of keeping the rules. If you don't form this intention, then we on our side are entitled to regard you as an enemy, and we would be entitled also – although we may not actually do this – to withdraw the benefits that make up our side of the bargain. If you are not willing even to try to keep the rules, why should we be willing to feed you, house you, look after you when you are ill, and so on? Perhaps on reflection, or after some experience in which society does not support you in this way, you will change your mind.'

This is a last-ditch defence. If after this we still have people who are not going to agree, we have to decide what to do. Arguably we might in fact withdraw from our side of the bargain, and cut off supplies until they come to their senses. At least we will mark them down, in some formal way, as actual or potential enemies of the system – in effect, as outlaws. For that is what they are, that is how they have positioned themselves, and the only educational move left to us is to show them the natural consequences of so positioning themselves. To try to cover this up, to pretend to ourselves and to them that they are still good contractual members of the institution, is merely to deceive everybody. They are parasitical, and must be shown to be such. Only a vague fear of being labelled 'authoritarian' or 'tough-minded' could prevent us from taking such measures.

As we have presented them, all these moves are bound to seem over-simplified, and it must be understood that almost everything depends on the way in which they are made – on the teacher-pupil relationships in general, the home background, and so on. We know this already, but it is no excuse for shirking the task of trying to bring out, in some clearly formalized way, the logical points that underlie such moves.

Sanctions and punishment

In the previous two sections we have tried to say something about the necessity for framing, communicating and enforcing a clearly defined contract, and the arguments which might be used to persuade pupils to adopt it. But to some people in some institutions, our discussion of rules and contracts may seem somewhat academic. The educators may have difficulty in maintaining even a minimum of law and order. So it is worth taking a close look at the notions of sanctions and punishment.

First, it is important that the teacher has the right view of punishment to begin with. Specific punishments, sanctions or penalties are unpleasant things that are meted out by the authorities to people living in a rule-governed system for specific breaches of the rules. It is part of the concept of a rule, in such a system, that a penalty normally follows the breaking of it – if it did not, there would be no rule but just a pious hope. So we must not look on punishment as something that a 'progressive' or 'liberal' teacher would avoid because it is unpleasant or nasty – it is *meant to be* nasty. That is what punishment is, and that is what you have to have if there are to be rules at all. Equally, punishment must not stem from the vindictive or angry feelings of the teacher or other authority. It is nothing to do with feelings at all; it is simply a logical consequence of rule-breaking.

This essential *impersonality* of punishment must be communicated to the pupils, so that they do not have the excuse of pretending that punishment is just 'them', the authorities, taking it out on 'us', the pupils. Obviously the more the authorities can co-operate with the pupils in framing the contract and the sanctions, the better. They can say in effect, 'Look, let's see what rules we need. OK, we need rules X, Y and Z. Now, we all know that we are often impulsive,

131

angry, selfish, lazy and so on, so what punishments do we need to attach to these rules to make sure they *are* rules, to make sure they are kept?' (Often the pupils will make better suggestions than the teachers.) Then when rules are broken, the teacher will not have to pose as a flouted authority, a person or pseudo-god whose will has been challenged; that is to play into the hands of the pupils' own immaturity. We have somehow to get them past the stage of conducting mimic battles of rebelling against 'authority' in the shape of parent-figures who have to be challenged. We have to avoid taking the role that the pupils' immaturity wants us to take, the role of the irate parent. We have rather to say something like, 'Oh, gosh, you've broken such-and-such a rule, what a pity you couldn't keep it. Well now, that means you have to do or suffer so-and-so, as we agreed in the contract, doesn't it?' Of course it is equally important that at *other* times, i.e. when not simply enforcing the contract, the teacher should appear (so to speak) more as a human being – as someone who is sometimes angry, and gets bored or resentful, though for most of the time (we hope) is quite fond of the pupils and will relate to them, be trusted by them and so on. The important thing is to *dissociate* the contract system from these personal considerations. Our pupils have to learn that rules and punishments are necessary, *not* because adults want them, but because any form of human life logically requires them. Just as we distinguish between the judge as a person and the judge as a law-enforcer, so they must learn to distinguish between the teacher as a person and the teacher in the role of rule-keeper or umpire.

The specific forms of punishment that we choose must, of course, be effective in ensuring that the rules are kept, and it is for this reason that they must be unpleasant. (If they were pleasant, breaking the rules would be rewarded and they would no longer be rules forbidding so-and-so but rules encouraging people to do so-and-so.) Precisely which forms of punishment are effective in this way, for which types of people, is of course an empirical question on which we cannot pronounce. All that is important here is to keep *this* mode of dealing with pupils – the mode of *deterring* – clearly distinct from other modes. For instance, as well as deterring a person we should also want him or her to make restitution, since as we saw earlier the sincere acceptance of a contract involves a person's being willing to make up for the damage or trouble he or she has caused by breaking it. But what we should say is not, 'You have deliberately broken Johnny's watch, which cost him a lot of money and trouble to get. I'll punish you by making you buy a new one.' For here we have muddled up two modes. Making him buy a new one may be no good as a deterrent: maybe the pupil is rich enough not to care or, if he is really sorry, he may genuinely want to make up for it by buying a new one. What we should say is, 'You've deliberately broken the watch. Now, by the rules, you must be deterred in some way to stop you doing that sort of thing again' (and here perhaps we give him lines or do something else that he doesn't like), 'and, which is quite different, since it's your fault that Johnny has not got a watch any more, the least you can do is to buy a new one.' Both these can be enforced, but they are different. Again, if a pupil is grossly lazy and consequently gets behind in her work, we want her to stop being lazy, and to catch up with her work. It *may* be that keeping her in detention does both of these, but not necessarily. We have to be clear what we are doing.

Armed with this clarity, by which practical knowledge and experience can be translated into effectiveness, the teacher should find it easier both to maintain discipline and to communicate the rules-and-contract system to the pupils. Nevertheless, much of what we have said may still seem very impractical. A teacher, particularly if teaching in a 'tough' or badly disciplined school, may be disposed to say, 'It's all very well telling us to enforce this contract, but *how*? We're often not allowed to apply certain sanctions (for instance corporal punishment). Indeed, sometimes we can't defend ourselves against some young thugs. Again, you tell us to persuade them to accept the contract, but some of them just *won't*, and what are we to do then? If we make all these rules and contracts very clear, as you suggest, and then can't enforce them, won't we just look sillier than ever?'

These are very fair points. We do believe that clarity and the moves we have been recommending would reduce the brute problem of maintaining law and order, particularly if this approach were adopted towards children from their earliest years. But we are not starry-eyed enough to believe that there will not be resisting cases. About these we can only add the following.

We are talking here about pupils who are, quite overtly and deliberately, opposed to the institution and its teachers; who have not made the move of accepting any sort of contract; who are predisposed not to agree, or to obey, at all. It is important that the teacher should identify these cases clearly, and not confuse them with the different cases of pupils who do, basically, accept the contract but (for various psychological reasons) find it difficult to keep. It is equally important for the teacher, having identified them, to be clear that this is, in effect, war, and a war that the teachers cannot afford to lose. They cannot afford to lose, not only because there is chaos in the school and teaching suffers, or because the particular contract that defines the school as an institution is being flouted, but also because this is, for the pupil, a model or archetypal case, and his or her attitude to and understanding of other future contracts will be determined by what happens here. Thus it is strictly for educational reasons, not for considerations of convenience, that the pupils must not be allowed to get away with it. Hence there is one move the teacher must not make: he or she must not back down, accept defeat, make some sort of compromise for the sake of a quiet life, or pretend the problem does not exist.

If it is war, what weapons does the teacher have? We omit here the various common sanctions that are used: detention, reporting to the headteacher and so on. We assume that other sanctions or pseudo-sanctions that the teacher may summon up, such as the pressure of the peer group or the backing of the pupils' parents, do not work either; nor does anything the teacher can do by way of informal relations with the pupil, in or out of school; nor does anything the official experts (the educational psychologist, the probation officer, etc.) can do. Next we assume that certain types of sanctions, which the teacher thinks might work (e.g. corporal punishment), are forbidden by the (possibly misguided) higher authorities. Finally, we assume that the teacher cannot ensure that the recalcitrant pupils are removed from the school and sent to some other institution. There remain two general lines of action.

First, the teacher, with the co-operation of the other teachers, can invent new sanctions of a different type. He or she can say, 'Look, I just cannot do my job, because I am not allowed to enforce certain rules, rules that I consider to be absolutely essential for any effective teaching, on certain pupils. Very well. I regard these pupils as wholly at war with us. If I can, I shall make sure that they pass no examinations, and also that they are regarded as unemployable – we are preparing a list of such pupils, which we shall circulate to employers and others. If the state or other authorities force me to make certain moves, such as standing in front of a class and teaching them, allowing them to sit for examinations, etc., then I shall make these moves; but I will do it in the most inefficient and incompetent manner possible. Anyway, I assure you that, if I am not given the necessary powers, parental backing, etc., these pupils will certainly suffer in their careers. Very likely they may become real criminals, in which case they will be a burden on society in general and the police in particular.' We have no doubt that determined teachers, acting in co-operation, could make this work effectively. Secondly, the school can simply arrange that the pupils who are at war should spend the whole of the time under conditions different from the other pupils. This would, in effect, be to produce a 'detention wing', or a mini-Borstal, within the school – something that, if the higher authorities will not arrange it outside the school, teachers can arrange for themselves.

All this would, of course, be highly regrettable and naturally nobody wants it to come to that. We should hope that by clarity in rule-making, by participation, by kindness, good staff – pupil relationships, parental support, etc. such cases would not arise. But – and it is a big but – it is better that they should be seen to arise, and be dealt with along these lines, than that we should pretend that they do not exist. It is far from uncommon – even in the 'best' schools – for there to be a sort of muted war between staff (or one or two members of the staff) and pupils (or some pupils). This must, at all costs, be brought into the open rather than muffled.

We have to remember that we are talking only about *one* mode of dealing with our pupils. None of what we have suggested here should be taken as implying that we should not *also* adopt the methods of the friend, the elder sibling or even the psychotherapist, as well as those of the judge and the police officer. Naturally, if the former methods are effectively deployed, the latter will be unnecessary. But both are valid. The important thing is to keep them distinct, and to use them both with a clear understanding. We now turn our attention to the general educational methods that might help pupils to grasp these points, and that, we hope, might obviate some of the more extreme difficulties we have been considering.

Rule-and-contract teaching in general

GENERAL METHODOLOGY

It is helpful to regard rule-and-contract systems as being in certain important respects like games (although the analogy breaks down at some points), particularly perhaps for children, who are more familiar with the notion of a game than with the wider notion of a contract. The game analogy is especially useful in helping the pupils to grasp some of the points made in earlier sections of this part, e.g. the *variety* of possible contracts, the idea that contracts and rule-governed activities have a *purpose*, that rules can be changed to carry out the purpose more efficiently, and various points about 'authority'. So we do not think the teacher should hesitate to use the analogy to the full.

There will be three basic types of context in which the teacher will try to get these points across:

1. An '*academic*' context, in which the points are made in a general form – perhaps roughly in the way we have made them here, suitably altered for different kinds of pupils.
2. The use of *examples*: 'real-life' examples or simulation situations, illustrations from the pupil's own experience (e.g. is there a 'contract' in his or her family life?) or a study of examples from history, legal cases and actual contracts (e.g. between worker and employer).
3. A context of *participation*. Here the pupils take part in framing and keeping contracts and sets of rules (as a school council, in arranging a dance or an outing, etc.).

We want to stress that all these are important and none is sufficient by itself. The third context is perhaps especially to be encouraged in schools and other institutions, because it is only in a participation situation that pupils will clearly see the 'pay-off', the actual results of making or breaking particular rules. It is essential to put responsibility firmly on the pupils themselves, because otherwise it really does become no more than a game to them, in the sense that it is not taken seriously. (This is, of course, the merit especially claimed for such methods as those used by the Outward Bound authorities, the 'summer camps' in the USA, and so on.) But equally, unless the academic context and examples are also used, the learning that is supposed to accrue from such situations will not be generalized, and hence not transferred to other rule-governed situations. (A child may see the point of rules in mountain-climbing, but not necessarily be helped thereby to see the point of rules in school or factory.) The academic or conceptual teaching, together with real-life examples, literary illustrations, acted-out situations, etc., is essential if the pupils are to develop true understanding.

CONTEXTS AND EXAMPLES

The academic points have been made already. We list here a random selection of contexts and examples for use with the other points.

1. Non-directive out-of-school situations, not centred on a particular task, in which a great deal of responsibility is placed on pupils for building social rules virtually from scratch (e.g. summer camps, survival situations, 'desert island' situations, like that in *Lord of the Flies*, and so on).

2. Specific out-of-school tasks that the pupils can be responsible for (school outings, arranging entertainments, organizing voluntary service, running a shop or a small-scale business enterprise).

3. In-school situations where pupils can be given practice in organizing and participating (the actual teaching and learning of a subject, school assemblies, school councils, arrangements for catering, cleaning, decorating, repairing, building, etc.).

4. Simulated situations or games that can be played with a particular task in mind for the group (e.g. a murder trial, conducting a political campaign), or with no particular group-function, but concentrating rather on the political and social rules that the group may evolve (the 'desert island' case).

5. Descriptions and discussion of clear and problematic cases of contract-keeping and contract-breaking, in history, literature or law.

6. Use of a wide variety of different contexts requiring different rules, particularly those varying on the dimension between 'instant obedience' and 'democratic discussion' (e.g. being in the army, serving as the crew of a sailing-ship or as a nurse on the one hand; being on a committee or deciding something with one's friends on the other). Role-playing in these different contexts is an obvious technique.

7. Exchanging roles, particularly those that the pupils find difficult to grasp in the abstract, or about which they have prejudices (e.g. making the pupil act as the teacher, the supervisor, the janitor, a police officer, etc.).

8. Accustoming the pupils to different social rituals or conventions (an old-fashioned dance, an unusual religious service, etc.).

9. Accustoming the pupils to different power structures (dictatorship, oligarchy, etc.) in contexts that are microcosms of such regimes.

10. Accustoming the pupils to different decision procedures (throwing dice, obeying a single person, voting, letting the most vocal or the strongest have their own way, etc.).

WHAT THE PUPILS MUST NOTICE

Here is a selection of questions that pupils should be encouraged to raise and answer in all these contexts and in such others as the teacher may devise.

1. In this (rule-governed) situation, where does the authority lie? In the will of a person or group? In written rules? Unwritten expectations?

2. What, in detail, *are* the rules governing this situation?

3. What sanctions attach to them? Are these specified, or do they consist of the general disapproval of other people? Are the sanctions enforced?

4. Are any of the rules ambiguous or vague? Is it clear what is to count as (for example) 'obscene' or 'tending to corrupt'?

5. Do the rules fulfil their purpose? Are they reasonable and requisite?

6. What is the *point* of this 'game' or rule-governed system? Is it something we engage in for its own sake, like a real game, or is it supposed to result in some kind of product (as discussions are supposed to result in truth, or social rules to result in social convenience)?

7. How would one make restitution for breaches of particular rules? What sort of damage is done by such breaches? What is the expenditure of time or trouble?

8. What temptation does one feel to break rule X or Y?

9. What temptation does one feel to dislike the rules in general,

and rebel against them? Or to be over-anxious in conforming to them?

10. In rule-*making*, what temptation does one feel towards excessive strictness or excessive laxity?

We shall not talk here about the importance of the teacher using his or her own imagination, monitoring and objectifying all these teaching situations by videotape, making sure that the conceptual points are fully understood, and so on. We shall confine ourselves to pleading with him or her to be imaginative and bold, but also at all costs to be *definite*. Here too we are up against a good deal of fashionable talk about participation, pupil power, the democratic school, student protest and so on, which is as vague as it is boring. There is little point merely in encouraging the pupils to join in or participate. If it is not clear to them what they are supposed to be *learning*, some of the more sensible ones will prefer to stick to their academic textbooks. Boldness is required primarily in using new contexts of teaching (for instance, out-of-school non-directive situations, rather than academic discussion), but the teacher then needs to go back again and again over the particular context, discussing it, making the pupils 're-play' it, recording it, having outside observers comment on it, and so on. We must ensure that the pupils are not having a good (or bad) time. We owe it to them that they should *learn*.

Suggestions for Further Reading

There is an immense amount of literature in this field and – apart from the impossibility of providing the reader with a complete list of relevant works – it may be most helpful if we list a few books that seem to us most likely to be of use.

The best and briefest book on the concept of authority is E.D. Watt's *Authority* (Croom Helm, London, 1982). This contains all the references needed for the philosophy of the topic.

The close connections between authority and moral education are made clear in John Wilson's *New Introduction to Moral Education* (Cassell, London, 1990), which also includes many useful references to relevant literature.

The connections with education in general emerge best in three books: *The Logic of Education* by P.H. Hirst and R.S. Peters (Routledge, London, 1970), *Education: an Introduction* by H. Loukes *et al*. (Martin Robertson, Oxford, 1983) and *Taking Education Seriously* by John Wilson and Barbara Cowell (Althouse Press, London, Ontario, 1989).

It is hard to know what to recommend in the general area of psychology and sociology. Standard and well-known works by Piaget, Freud, Adorno, Weber, Durkheim and others are of course well worth reading, but the most useful modern book is perhaps *Madness and Modernity* by C.R. Badcock (Blackwell, Oxford, 1983).

Index